Praise for the Author

I have known Katrina since our time working together on a far northwestern Queensland mining project, which required both FIFO and Head Office coordination. Katrina demonstrated her highly organised strategic logistical and onboarding/offboarding skills to ensure not only the effective management of the project but to safeguard the mental health of the team's greatest asset… our staff.

Katrina's commitment to the team and project coordination skills resulted in her undertaking a FIFO role to further ensure the smooth and effective management of the project.

Nicole Shillington
Senior Contracts Manager, Abu Dhabi Airport

Katrina Wilson is both a childhood friend and former employee of mine. I brought her into HRI to 'herd the cats' (the site-based project engineering team) on our Drilling Rig Construction Projects in Ulsan, South Korea.

Katrina demonstrated her great organisational, diplomatic and adaptive skills to integrate into an established project team and implement an administrative battle rhythm that ensured everyone was paid and logistically supported in South Korea.

Justin Nally
General Manager, Horizon Resources International

I have had the privilege of working with Katrina Wilson in helping to promote research across the university where we work. Katrina has built on her highly developed intelligence and intuition to design and implement support systems that work effectively from a whole-of-organisation perspective.

She asks regularly, "How does this work?" and "Why are we doing this?" Addressing these questions has enhanced the efficiency of our operations and has maximised the productivity of our colleagues.

The expertise, commitment and business as usual approach I have seen Katrina demonstrate lead me to be assured that the principles of her RUGBY Mindset and Quality Review system, successfully deployed, will enhance any business.

Professor Patrick Danaher
PhD

Drawing on her extensive expertise as a project manager and administrator, Katrina has produced a highly readable and insightful book, enriched by thought-provoking and relatable anecdotes. In sharing the RUGBY framework which she has developed, Katrina delivers a practical and highly valuable business tool.

Melissa McKain
DipT, BBus, GradDipAppSci

RUGBY
Mindset & Quality Review®

GLOBAL
PUBLISHING
G R O U P

Global Publishing Group
Australia • New Zealand • Singapore • America • London

RUGBY

Mindset & Quality Review®

Redefining Business Performance and Competitive Edge

Katrina M Wilson

First Edition 2017

National Library of Australia

Cataloguing-in-Publication entry:

Creator: Wilson, Katrina M. author.

Title: Rugby Mindset & Quality Review : Redefining Business Performance and Competitive Edge / Katrina M Wilson.

ISBN: 9781925288544 (paperback)

Subjects: Personnel management.
Executive coaching.
Employee empowerment.
Delegation of authority.
Organizational behavior.
Organizational change.
Employee motivation.
Success in business.

Published by Global Publishing Group
PO Box 517 Mt Evelyn, Victoria 3796 Australia
Email info@GlobalPublishingGroup.com.au

Printed in China

For further information about orders:
Phone: +61 3 9739 4686 or Fax +61 3 8648 6871

A very special thank you to my wonderfully supportive parents Leo and Judy Wilson – who have always encouraged me to write – although I am not sure a business book related to quality is what you had in mind!

My second mother and longest friend Helen. I love the place I have in your heart, your family and your home.

Louise Ross for taking the time to read my first manuscript – your impartial review and support has been truly appreciated because you offered your genuine opinion and feedback.

Dr Rolf Gomes for sharing your story and the vision of Heart of Australia.

Delena Brophy Farmer and Paul Blackburn for sharing your knowledge and experiences as specialists and for your contribution in the 'Inverse Lottery' chapter.

I thank the many people who have endured my focus and self-imposed isolation as I developed RUGBY and wrote this book. I thank my brothers and sisters Stephen, Peta-Mary, Andrew, Alyce, Carol and Jocelyn and my friends whose company I have enjoyed sporadically.

EXTRA BONUS

The RUGBY Mindset and Quality Review team are keen to reinvigorate quality review and quality management systems in your business, project or workplace and look forward to introducing an agile marketing and technology approach to support next level thinking in the quality game.

To access any of the electronic tools and resources which have been developed to support small business and this book, or to have a one-on-one conversation please contact us at...

www.TheRugbyMindset.com

or simply scan the QR code above or on the front of the book!

A conversation costs nothing – so your first conversation is free.

Acknowledgements

This book would never have had legs if not for the people who have mentored, counselled and supported me as I navigated through my human errors and career challenges. I extend a very big thank you and recognition to the following people who have helped turn me out to be the professional I am today.

Thank you Kerry O'Dea for demonstrating, with the ethic you apply to everything that you do, that attention to detail and a quality result is never time wasted.

Thank you Bill Thomson, professional mentor and friend. You sir, lead with the best example. I have observed your integrity, strength, strategy and compassion, all traits I try to emulate each and every day.

Thank you Tony Reynolds. You at first terrified me and then surprised me with your warmth and genuine character. You shared your knowledge and experience generously, and introduced to me your remarkable perspective of approaching everything with a different focus and to always 'give it a go'. Thank you for your curiosity. Thank you for your mentorship. Thank you for your friendship.

Thank you Stephen Nally for affording me the opportunity to work in South Korea with the Horizon Resources International and Diamond Offshore Drilling team – my pinnacle project role to date. It was while working with you and the team, on this project and in a foreign country that I experienced some of my greatest challenges and development opportunities and cemented for me the benefits of RUGBY Quality Review as a business process loop to support a continual improvement agenda.

Thank you Mark Butlin for changing my career direction with one phone call. Your opportunity to interview for the job I now enjoy, not only provided me with an income stream, but offered me the opportunity to reground myself for a little while. Had I never worked at a university and instead continued to work in major project delivery, and had people who research and write as a passion not surrounded me as they earnt a crust academically, I would never have cast a thought towards writing a book. Thank you – this book is a direct result of your phone call.

A final and most heartfelt thank you to my friend Ryan. Our kinship and shared experiences as we matured personally and professionally in Australia and in South Korea is something that I treasure. I look forward to many more conversations and experiences with the young man who epitomises the words brave and responsible for me.

Contents

Foreword

When I first delved into this work, I thought it did not have any relevance to my one-man business but the deeper I dug, the more relevant I found it. If there is only one of you, you had better make sure you make the most of everything you have ever produced.

Certainly, I empathise with the 'wait staff' – waiter/waitress here in northern England – who retained only the details of the unfinished business whilst instantly forgetting the overfed customer whose credit card had just been transacted.

I am sure my business would move forward in leaps and bounds if I were to adopt a hierarchical cadence of reviewing and improving all aspects of the business rather than proving to myself daily what a hero I am by sitting at my desk until I fall asleep. Or, realising that I have not retained a single word from the last five contractual documents I have been reading. Worse, losing consciousness whilst typing and waking to find 200 pages comprising entirely the letter v.

What I always find remarkable when I read work such as this is just how many management techniques are transferrable between vastly differing industries.

At first glance, there would seem to be little commonality between a mobile cardiologist clinic and a mine in the outback, but they share the common attribute that they both contribute massively to the wellbeing of individuals directly involved and to the wider community whose success and sustainability is dependent upon a diverse range of successful activity.

Katrina's work reminded me of my collection of 1959 Agfa Super Silette Automatic cameras. To the uninitiated, they are identical, but I know them as individuals – the one with the stiff focusing ring, another with a faulty rangefinder and one with a broken spring on the film transport mechanism.

Yet it is precisely these imperfections, which make my collection interesting and valuable (just to me). It is the same with businesses. They are nearly all running on a broken wheel because they are run by human beings. And they are the best ones. Some are run by computers and they really are in trouble.

So, I hope that as you get absorbed into Katrina's ideas, you will see the places where your business needs to take up RUGBY and not just assume it's for all the other companies.

Perhaps you are already earning good profits. Good, then take heed of Katrina's ideas and spend less time earning those profits. On the other hand, perhaps you think you do not have time to adopt the RUGBY approach. If so, maybe you are fighting the Battle of Stamford Bridge (the one in Yorkshire in 1066, not the recent game between Chelsea and Arsenal) and do not have time to listen to the salesman from the Acme Machine Gun Company.

I know that Katrina will not mind my revealing that I have enjoyed breakfast with her on several occasions. And let me disabuse you of the vast extrapolation of the relationship between Katrina and myself which your imagination is right now entertaining.

The breakfasts were taken at 4 am during 24 hr periods of site investigations in a major container terminal under the directions of an eminent judge in a civil engineering dispute.

Katrina oversaw logistics planning with the aim of keeping a collection of international engineering experts and lawyers representing different parties in a dispute from inflicting grievous bodily harm on each other.

In the main, she succeeded in this – the attrition rate was in single percentage figures – and I am sure that the challenges, which she faced, provided the germ of an idea that her subsequent experiences moulded into this book.

Katrina is a one-off – a true outlier in business. I hope you enjoy the read as much as I did.

John Knapton
November 2016

How to Enjoy This Book

It is not shocking to read that the statistics for someone to read a business book from front to back cover is low.

Let's face it, business books are not page turners. There are usually no characters for us to form any kind of affinity or relationship with and they are usually written in a style of people telling us what we should and should not do – if we want to be successful.

So why do we purchase a business book if we never read it from cover to cover? We purchase them because we have identified a need to improve something about ourselves or our business and we are looking for solutions.

We don't finish reading a business book or we put it on the shelf for another day, because we forget that we are the solution to resolve whatever challenges us, and we never found the solution we were looking for in the first three chapters of the book. Some of us are still searching for solutions.

I don't believe that any one business book is ever going to be able to tell us what we need to do to overcome our challenges because our skills and passion, our experience, our business and our style are unique to each of us.

I do believe that in every business book published, in every author's experience, there is an exceptional effort made, and information contained within, that will lend some perspective towards us finding our own solution.

This book falls outside the shape or structure a business book usually takes. In fact, this book now has very little structure about it at all – because you can, and will need to, draw your own conclusions.

It is a book that you can pick up at any time, open at any page, and read about an experience that you may relate to or a concept or an innovative approach you may want to apply to your business and it has been structured to capture the process you can follow, to shape your own practical application of these observations to suit your business or personal business style.

This book is about providing reflection opportunities captured from my own and others' experiences over many years.

This book is about you finding your own solution to the challenges you face, and introducing to you an innovative approach to total quality management, a RUGBY Mindset approach and RUGBY Quality and Review process, that aligns sound business practices that you probably already use, to achieve, maintain and succeed in your business.

As you read, please don't just look for a solution to a problem or challenge that you are currently experiencing – remember that *you* are the solution to resolve what challenges you.

Laugh with me at some of the ridiculous situations I have found myself in, because I did not take five minutes to be situationally aware enough to challenge my own prejudices and norms.

Shake your head with resignation and take a moment in extending empathy towards my previous employers for mistakes made – and take a moment to think about any other learnings my employers and I might have gained from these mistakes.

Recognise with me, that comfort, familiarity, prejudices and overconfidence closes our eyes to the potential of positive change or influence, and that we should always look towards situational awareness and understanding first.

Most of all, I would like for you to enjoy reading some of the amazing experiences, employment opportunities and environmental exposures I've benefited from and perhaps benefit from them as I have, by identifying your point of difference, your competitive edge, your strengths and weaknesses, and most specifically, what makes you a unique human in the workplace.

Enjoy!

> *"Comfort, familiarity, prejudice and overconfidence closes our eyes to the potential of positive change. Always look towards understanding first."*
>
> **Katrina Wilson**

Introduction

The concept of RUGBY Quality Review was developed to draw out and identify the hidden failures that exist in business before they require critical response or result in a critical risk or loss.

RUGBY Quality Review developed from my experience of quality management practices in the workplace, and to support all business owners and quality managers who struggle daily to maintain the right focus towards the quality and quality management practices that are so essential for a business to grow and be successful.

One of the most significant issues that challenge businesses today, is our understanding of the purpose and intent of quality management practices – the very reason they have been developed in the first place.

We overlook an ailing process or documentation as we attend to our business as usual – because *if it's not broken… we don't fix it.*

For the most part, quality in business and the management practices that are supposed to support it, usually has its strongest focus when a business or project applies scrutiny to it – when an external accrediting body has been engaged to reaccredit our business or when something has gone wrong.

It's at this time you see business owners and quality managers starting to sweat bullets, as they try to gather the information to support their reaccreditation or mitigate their risk and exposure when something has gone wrong.

It is to this purpose that RUGBY Quality Review was developed – for a business to start using its already engaged talent base – its employees – to redefine quality management practices in their business with the result being a competitive edge.

RUGBY Quality Review has its foundation in a very successful site safety practice identified using red, green, blue and yellow tagging on electrical equipment. Its success is in its very transparency. The practice itself has a visual cue attached to a potentially dangerous physical object – a tag that is either red, green, blue or yellow – and it creates a symbiotic relationship between a human's response to something that has potential to harm or catastrophically kill – to what some may perceive to be a seemingly harmless object.

Tagging electrical equipment with a red, green, blue and yellow tag is successful on site, because there is a very clear understanding of what the visual cues mean and how we are expected to respond to it.

Non-compliance or lack of recognition and incorrect response to the visual cues on site could mean you are no longer employed on site because you have not only exposed yourself to unnecessary risk, but others as well. It's that black and white. If you don't respond as the visual cue requires, you could find yourself at best unemployed or at worst contributing towards harming yourself or others.

The same applies in the visual cues we have available to us in our everyday life, for example when you drive a vehicle.

You can drive a motor vehicle because you have been trained to operate that piece of machinery, you have passed the test that measures your competence against the minimum standard required to safely operate that piece of machinery, and you have demonstrated your understanding of the traffic rules and regulations you must and are legally required to adhere to.

All of these things, our experience and training, our understanding of the traffic rules and regulations and our ability to competently and safely navigate from point A to point B come undone as soon as we introduce some human agency into the equation – as soon as we start thinking only of ourselves and not of *ourselves and others*.

If we don't respond to the visual cue of a red traffic signal and stop, if we choose instead to accelerate and proceed contrary to the required response

– we are not only putting ourselves at risk of an accident which could result in injury or death, we are also exposing others to an unnecessary risk.

It's not like a traffic signal moves immediately from green to red. A traffic light moves from green *to amber* to red – traffic is managed *the world over* using the same signals and visual cues. If the traffic light is green – you can proceed. If the traffic light is amber – you decelerate and prepare to stop. If the traffic light is red – you stop. Easy.

Things get messy and potentially catastrophic when one driver chooses not to respond with the required behaviour or response. It only takes one person to change the outcome of something that should have been successful to navigate and easy to follow. Only one thing needs to change for everything to change. Why?

Because as one person is choosing to ignore the required response at an intersection and accelerating or proceeding through a red traffic light – another is responding at the same intersection to accelerate and proceed from a green traffic light.

RUGBY Quality Review has been developed to be a business's amber traffic signal – its amber alert. It's that time somewhere between go and stop, that pivotal period in business where a human will demonstrate agency – and it is this period in business where our greatest risk occurs – because we as human beings tend to think of ourselves first before we think of others.

This process was developed because I had time to develop it. For the early part of 2015, I was unemployed, so I had a lot of time on my hands to think – but many of us don't have the luxury of time. Many of us don't have the mindset or discipline to capture time either – we are always busy and focused elsewhere in our busy and distracted life.

Quality is something that should be easily achieved and maintained – because we all take pride in doing something to the best of our ability – but it's not.

RUGBY Quality Review should be an easy process to develop and maintain in your business – but it won't be – because whilst the process itself is as transparent as the appropriate and required response to traffic signals at an intersection or the application of red, green, blue and yellow tags to electrical equipment on site, our human behaviours in the workplace will always prevail to obstruct.

This is why I cast some thought towards shaping a mindset that would support the success of RUGBY Quality Review – because one of the first responses you will hear when you ask someone to review quality practices is "I don't have time for that" or "I will do it when I get time". Let me translate this for you. *"It's not a priority for me right now."*

No one will ever find time for something that they consider to be a low priority – think about it, if something was important and considered a priority there would be no need to find time in the first place.

RUGBY Mindset is about reinforcing the message that quality is a priority for your business's success. If a business owner or manager places no value or priority on quality management practices, then an employee won't either – and this is one of the critical elements a business must demonstrate and evidence as it seeks certification. No external certification body will endorse and support through certification a business that doesn't place value on the product that they are selling – quality standards.

To address the challenge of time-poor responses RUGBY Quality Review has captured the potential to realise the time in your business using a 'battle rhythm' and has been massaged to align with the team sport of rugby to provide a vernacular in your business. Even if you don't follow the sport itself, you most probably support a team in sport – and you have a concept of what a successful team looks like and what an unsuccessful team looks like.

The mindset is about recognising behaviours such as bystander apathy, where we consciously choose to not be involved in something, or in the workplace, choosing to consider it someone else's job or fiercely defending ourselves if someone thinks it is **our job**. The mindset is about encouraging people to 'get some skin in the game' to use a sporting analogy – to choose to be involved.

RUGBY Mindset and Quality Review is about recognising, as John Knapton particularly notes in his foreword, that mistakes are always going to be made because humans populate the workplace.

It is about recognising the pivot points where our human agency influences our business, and focusing towards lowering how recurrently, easily preventable and costly mistakes arise in business as we contribute in the business towards the group development model of forming-storming-norming and performing.

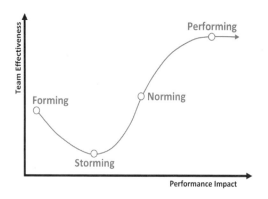

Forming	The team act as individuals and there is a lack of clarity about the team's purpose and individual roles.
	Behaviour: Team acquaints and establishes ground rules.
Storming	Members start to communicate their feelings but still view themselves as individuals rather than part of the team. They resist control by group leaders and show hostility.
	Behaviour: Conflict arises as people begin to establish their place in the team.

Norming   There is a level of consensus and agreement within the team. There is clarity about individual roles.

The role of the leader is important in managing this.

Behaviour: People feel part of the team and realise that they can achieve work if they accept other viewpoints.

Performing   The group has a clear strategy and shared vision. It can operate autonomously and resolve issues positively.

Behaviour: The team works in an open and trusting atmosphere where flexibility is the key and hierarchy is of little importance.

> *"RUGBY Mindset and Quality Review is about getting some skin in the quality game."*
>
> **Katrina Wilson**

SECTION 1

Warm Up

CHAPTER 1

Opening as it Closes

This book opens as it closes, as it captures two observations that literally 'fell out' as I sought to identify the advantageous 'business as usual' workplace behaviours that would support effective implementation of RUGBY Quality Review in business, and also to identify the restraining 'business as usual' workplace behaviours that would challenge its potential and success.

My vision for RUGBY Quality Review is as bold as the vision that Bill Gates set when he envisioned 'A computer on every desk and in every home' – and we all know how well that turned out.

My vision is to have this very simple review process effectively implemented and maintained in every business and for every employee to be valued and recognised for their unique contributions in their workplace. It is a bold ambition – but a vision starts with an outrageous end in mind.

I was reluctant to place these observations and experiences at the front of the book, because I wrote the book to promote to businesses, the concept of RUGBY Quality Review and the collaborative business as usual mindset that supports it, a RUGBY Mindset – as a process that can be easily and practically applied into any workplace or project.

I was hesitant, because a reader could misinterpret the intent of my writing this book, as an indiscrete effort towards shameless self-promotion or hubris and (at worst) put the book down never to be touched again or (at best) use the book as a beer or wine coaster.

I am nervous about sharing these observations at the front of the book, because when I shared these observations with my 'test audience' I was actively participating in a conversation with people who either know me personally or with people who have worked with me, and therefore have some frame towards how I think and work. Within conversations with people I know, I have a history and a voice.

By placing these observations at the front of my book, I am humbly recognising two potential outcomes – one of which leaves my hard work and investment vulnerable.

I may isolate the potential of RUGBY Quality Review from you the employee, business leader or owner, whereby it is summarily dismissed out of hand, or I may garner your interest or curiosity.

I am hoping for the latter, because the disparity between a conversation and written form is wide – in written form, I have an audience who can get up and leave at any time – and I will never know the reason why.

The opening chapters of this book capture the two golden nuggets that fell out as I tested and challenged the integrity of RUGBY Quality Review, the outcome of which all research aspires – the identification of something that was not expected – and the concept of RUGBY Quality Review.

I have placed them in the front of the book, because I recognise that whilst the people that I shared RUGBY Quality Review with showed a genuine interest in the concept and process of this 'business as usual' quality practice, they were more curious about the observations I captured as I was challenging (read: trying to break) the agility and currency of the process for business.

So this book starts as it ends – capturing what people were most interested in – because I also know that most people don't read a book from cover to cover – unless it's a literary and imaginative masterpiece or thriller.

I do hope that you push through towards the end of the book however, as what is captured in between are the experiences, observations and processes that will provide relevance to the first three chapters of the book and also a frame of reference and vernacular that can support you as you begin to introduce RUGBY Quality Review into your business and business as usual practices.

> *"RUGBY Mindset and Quality Review is a collaborative business as usual mindset that supports a continual review and improvement process that can be easily and practically applied into any workplace or project."*
>
> **Katrina Wilson**

CHAPTER 2

One Golden Nugget

Adopting a RUGBY Mindset provides any person the opportunity to pause and credibly identify, interrogate and respectfully respond to behaviours that contribute towards conflict in a workplace.

This chapter is not going to make perfect sense to you until you have an opportunity to reflect upon some of the observations and experiences I have captured in the book.

Be patient, and remember that this golden nugget was something that fell out of the back of my business interrogation and authorship experience. *I did not even know it existed until the end.* This my friends, is a shared introduction to one of life's most charming experiences – that being one of delayed gratification.

What this chapter does draw together for you is the parallel between how we can successfully recognise the true conflicts in a workplace by positioning ourselves to credibly identify, and strategically respond to and stop, workplace conflicts when applying a RUGBY Mindset.

Conflicts do occur and will continue to occur in a workplace, because humans populate the workplace.

Humans – who are unique in the way they think and how they deliver on the job that they are paid to do, often contributing from an understanding and a value-set that has potential to not align with someone else's. This is what makes every workplace unique and challenging, and it is where many workplaces stumble.

Behaviours that contribute towards conflict in a workplace, if captured correctly and responded to appropriately, rarely present the opportunity for an unsubstantiated claim of bullying and harassment to raise its ugly profile. This is where many workplaces can flourish.

I want to be very careful in clarifying that this chapter does not seek to identify or address bullying in the workplace. Workplace bullying is such a serious issue that it has a legal definition applied to it. And, this is an excellent point to start in recognising that – workplace bullying has a legal definition.

Mention bullying in a workplace and people break a sweat and lose colour – because it is so very personal. A claim of bullying has the potential to impact on a person's career, not to mention their bread and butter if it is not correctly identified, addressed and responded to appropriately.

A claim of bullying has no merit until there is evidence to support it. It is not a nice thing to put in writing, but we all know someone out there in business, who make claim to workplace bullying when the real issue could be, amongst other things, that they are deflecting from doing the job they are paid to do.

This is what a RUGBY Mindset can assist with – helping the person who is responsible to identify and respond to the claim of bullying, by introducing an uncomplicated approach and a vernacular to identify and address the true issue or behaviour.

Mention bullying in a workplace and people respond with "Really?" as if it may not credibly exist – and in their mind it probably doesn't because they may enjoy a good relationship with the person who you claim to be a bully.

Here is the good news though – when personally presented with being either identified as a bully or having identified yourself as a target of a bully – if you start asking questions from a legally defined baseline – you can usually move towards a decision point, where you choose how you respond.

If you position yourself to make a decision in choosing how you respond from what is legally defined and identified as bullying, you have the opportunity to:

- Honourably reflect and identify if you yourself are in any way accountable, responsible or contributing towards a conflict in values or bullying behaviours and if you can remedy through conversation, mediation, training or further education.

- Be confident that the work that you deliver on and contribute towards, that you are accountable and responsible for, leaves your employer in a better position than before you contributed towards it – this makes you a competent employee that every business wants to employ.

- Verify the substance and validity of your claim. Recognise that it is unprofessional, irresponsible and morally reprehensible to make an unsubstantiated claim against another.

- Evidence to your manager the bullying behaviours that will support your claim. You need to do this if you are going to provide any credibility to your claim and capture the support you will need to proactively address the behaviour and environment.

- Provide your employer an opportunity to address the behaviour before it escalates. An unsubstantiated claim leads to further conflict, emotional turmoil or workplace compensation claims and/or legal proceedings.

Good employers hate losing competent employees more than they do addressing recalcitrant workplace behaviours. Be professional and mature in giving your employer the opportunity to respond.

- Choose your response to ensure success of your ultimate goal, which is to *return home to your family and friends at the end of every workday happy in health and state of mind*.

Every employee and employer has a right to expect that they will return home happy in health and state of mind and every employee has a responsibility to ensure that the work that they do ensures best practice for their employer.

Attend any workplace relationships course, and one of the combustion points that you will have identified to you when addressing negative workplace behaviours that lead to bullying, is that conflict itself starts because of a conflict in values. Where the values that you identify with, model, and will defend, directly conflict with the values that another identifies with, models, and will defend.

What any workplace will promote and spend a lot of time, money and resources in education and training is recognition, broadmindedness and resolution of the conflict in values. What they don't tell you is how you identify and then respond to these behaviours when you perceive yourself to be the subject and focus of negative attention or behaviours.

One of the last things I recognised as I challenged the integrity of RUGBY Quality Review, is that it provides a simple framework from which you can respond appropriately.

This chapter has been written to share with you how a RUGBY Mindset can assist you to confidently identify the negative workplace behaviours that contribute to conflict in the workplace, and the framework can provide to you the opportunity to pause and appropriately respond to the true issue at hand.

There are experts out there – people who successfully navigate the political quagmire of business and innately dance the subtle steps of conflict identification, negotiation and resolution.

I think these people successfully navigate the political business quagmire (and I offer a customer / service sales liaison as an example) because they are smart enough to ask themselves:

- What does the other person want as an outcome? What is their objective?

Every successful salesperson knows this – and they align their sales pitch towards a win–win. The customer gets the product that they want and the salesperson closes the sale.

- Can I provide the other person what they want as an outcome to achieve their objective?

Every successful salesperson knows this too – they will identify very quickly if what the customer wants is something that they have to offer. It has potential for a win–win or a lose–lose outcome. The outcome is hedged.

If it is not exactly what the customer wants (and let us be real – everyone always wants more for less) then a superb salesperson will take the opportunity to align their products as closely as they can to what the customer wants to close the sale.

- Does what the other person wants even exist?

Again, every resourceful salesperson knows this – you can't close a sale on something that you don't have to sell, or that doesn't even exist. Next customer!

- Should what the other person wants exist?

This is the point where innovation and future success can occur. Something new could be developed from this point – a new product or service could be introduced to your business or the market. You have just been provided *for free* an opportunity to develop further and profit from something, that until this point did not even exist or had not occurred to you.

This last point is where I think conflict in a workplace starts – because most people don't even consider this as a further option. If there is a need, there is a market – but this doesn't necessarily mean that one person's need reflects a market. Nevertheless, it should at least be considered and not dismissed out of hand.

You will not find any solution to workplace bullying within these pages, because addressing bullying starts personally. What you may find is that by approaching the workplace conflict, to recognise and identify the true issue with a RUGBY Mindset, that the conflict itself is just that – a conflict of values and not a weak claim to bullying.

You may find your shift towards a RUGBY Mindset could assist you in recalibrating your values compass towards understanding and broadmindedness, by identifying where your employer and your manager hold you accountable and responsible for contributing to the business, so that you can respectfully and confidently respond to the situation if required.

Adopting a RUGBY Mindset focused towards identifying account- abilities, responsibilities and contributions removes the identity of a bully and a victim from the workplace, by focusing on and addressing the behaviours that contribute to conflict.

> *"Remove the identity of a bully and a victim from the workplace by addressing the behaviours that contribute to conflict."*
>
> **Katrina Wilson**

How to Identify and Respond to Conflicting Values in Your Workplace

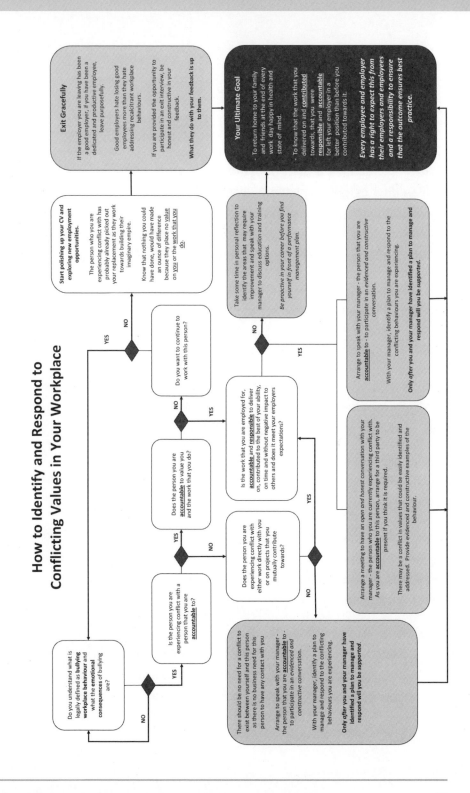

CHAPTER 3

Two Golden Nuggets

By implementing a 'battle rhythm' to capture the work that is identified by my employer as business as usual (specific to my role), by placing focus on executing the work that I am accountable and responsible for, I can on more days than not, knock those deliverables over in the opening hours of each business day.

When I shared this little golden nugget with business owners, leaders and managers, their initial response was one of disbelief and incredulity – no surprise there, it is a daring claim. Their second response was one of scepticism, and their third – curiosity.

They were curious to know what *I think I know* and they wanted to assess for themselves the validity of my claim. Thanks! I'd love to chat some time – I enjoy a nice full-bodied red…..

When I shared this little golden nugget with my peers, the people who I work with every day, their initial response was one of disbelief and incredulity – again, no surprise…

Their second response was to dismiss what I had just shared – they were not curious at all. Sigh! I guess my mother is right; "A prophet is never recognised in their hometown, amongst relatives and family." *Caveat: Never, at any point in time, have I ever considered myself a prophet!*

In fact, without exception, the third response I received from my peers was one of caution – "Don't let anyone else hear you say that – or you won't have a job". My peers were not misguided in their unsolicited advice – it was a response based on their perception of their workplace terrain and their perception of how productivity and excellence is recognised and rewarded in that environment – their workplace.

Although my peers were not at all curious, now I most certainly was… *"Oooohhhh – so it's a secret?"* Also, *"I could lose my job?"*

Interesting isn't it? Two very different responses from the same demographic – business. The thought leaders and business owners were looking to benefit from any thoughts or experience I might be able to provide them, and wanted to have a chat. My peers provided caution to cease and desist immediately.

So why was there such a polar response to my claim? There could be a myriad of reasons, but from all my time spent in rumination, I could only identify two:

- The business owners, leaders and managers saw potential to capture a **competitive edge** for their business or the work that they are accountable and responsible for in business and my peers saw… **redundancy**.

- The caution that my peers afforded me, with good intention, is not misplaced. It is a belief held by many, one that I regularly see in the workplace as an **employee** – if I don't look busy, if I don't tell everyone that I am busy, then a question exists as to how valuable I am as an employee. *Potentially, my job and livelihood is at stake.*

My peers were correct in identifying redundancy, because the way that I work actually *creates* redundancy in my job, something that I work doggedly towards achieving. Whilst my peers view redundancy despondently, I view redundancy as an opportunity *to profit* by saving time *not by saving money*.

If I can save time, whilst working towards achieving the minimum standard of work and output required by my employer (which is captured as my role description) then my employer and I can only ever profit.

I have worked as an **employee** and as a **contractor**, and as a contractor working on a project or within a business, it is irrelevant if you look busy or not. It is irrelevant if you tell everyone that you are busy – because as a contractor if you are not delivering on the job that you have been employed to do – *you will not have a job.*

As a contractor, you have been employed for a specific period to deliver on a specific element or deliverable of a project or business – if you are not doing your job – *someone else* will be employed to deliver on the job.

It is this understanding, having been employed for a number of years as a contractor, that has enabled me to be efficient in my workplace and has allowed me to capture time in my workday to value add in my role. It doesn't matter if I look busy, as long as *I am busy* delivering on the work that I have been employed to do and seeking to always improve the service and support I provide.

What is a battle rhythm?

If you ever find yourself across the dining table or work desk from a gentleman by the name of William McLeod Thomson – take pause to recognise *that* day has potential to be one of the luckiest days of your life. If you are speaking with the Bill I know, you are about to participate in a conversation that will respectfully challenge the way that you think.

I cannot say enough noble things about this guy – he is one of my professional mentors now, but he was once my boss – and he nurtured and trained me to be the consulting professional I am today.

Before I started working with Bill, I was an administrator working in an international consulting engineering design firm. Without question, I turned up to work each day and did the work that I was directed to focus on.

Under Bill's mentoring, I was trained to identify challenge and opportunities where others saw nuisance and adversity, and he taught me the discipline, benefits *and profit* of a successful battle rhythm.

Anyone with a military background will know what a battle rhythm is – because it is, amongst other things, a primary operational tactic used by militaries across the world. Centuries of campaigns have hinged on the success of a well-planned and executed battle rhythm.

One of the most recognised and successful military campaigners was Sun Tzu, a Taoist general, military strategist, and philosopher who lived in the period of 544–496 BCE in ancient China.

Contemporary business books continue to be written using Sun Tzu's military principles – and one of them was my first Christmas gift from Bill and his wife Alison.

It was a gift, because it would never have been a book that I would have picked up off the bookstore shelf in the first place.

The Art of War for Women by Chin-Ning Chu, is now a wellthumbed book in my personal library – I am sometimes curious as to the direction my career might have taken or that it may have perhaps even stalled, had I not received this gift. It is a curiosity explored without regret, because the one thing that Bill and Alison gave to me with that book was an enhanced ability to be strategic in my personal and business life.

My personal battle rhythm

Think and work differently to others

One of my first strategies in business is to think and work differently to others – *if there is a benefit or profit in doing so* – and it has its inception from reading and re-reading *The Art of War for Women*.

There are so many contemplative gems within the pages of *The Art of War for Women*, which is why this book is such as treasured and well-thumbed book in my personal library. The author has transcended time and gender, by taking an historical literary *military* capture from a revered historical author, Sun Tzu, and has applied real life examples and responses, which have been specifically tailored to support the female business leader, executive and professional of today.

The underlying message conveyed in this book, and where its message transcends time and gender, is that it is important to recognise that as individuals with our own unique personalities, experiences, skillset, education and passions, we all approach our work and focus our attention differently. Not necessarily better. Not necessarily worse. Differently. That is what makes our workplaces, successes and failures unique – because we bring into our workplace our strengths, weaknesses and experience.

The way I approach my work has its shape and focus not only from the training my mentors have beneficiated me; it has also been influenced through the very sequence of my employment and unemployment opportunities and from the people I have worked alongside.

Plan your work to deliver seamlessly

My personal battle rhythm starts where my workday finished the day before. Seamlessly.

Whilst many are exhaling a sigh as they close off their day and before they shut their computer off, I am preparing for what I am going to do the next day.

In the last half hour of my business day – **every day**, I review what I will be focusing and delivering on not only the next day, but also in the coming week, month and quarter. In doing so, I am continually reminding myself of my future work and am confident that there is limited potential to overlook something.

When I go home from work each day, I never give a thought to my employment until I return to work the next day. There is a recognised psychology in this behaviour. It's called the Zeigarnik Effect – *where people remember uncompleted or interrupted tasks better than completed tasks.*

I don't worry, stress or lose sleep on uncompleted or interrupted tasks, because at the close of each day I identify and plan for the work that stills needs to be completed in the future. *By doing this, I am shifting potentially unfinished business,* **unknowns** – *the things that I could lose sleep and worry over* – *into* **recognised and planned for knowns.**

This repetitive business discipline ensures that I refocus my priorities every day to identify what I still have to deliver on and allows me to recognise for a brief moment all of the work that I've completed that day and give myself a little pat on the back *before, as Zeigarnik's theory predicts, I forget about them and move on.*

Whilst many people, in the first hour of their business day, are lining up for their morning barista-made coffee to fortify them for the day ahead and sharing personal pleasantries with their peers as they wait, I am completing the tasks that I identified to deliver on the business day before. *Remember – my business day started in the last half hour of the day before.*

There are five very good reasons for this:

1. I know that my success of getting a barista-made coffee *quickly* significantly increases if I don't compete against the morning coffee crowd – and for that hour, my time is better spent focused elsewhere.

2. I already know what I am going to be focusing on that day, and I have an idea of how busy my day is going to be – I might not have time to grab that indulgent barista-made coffee.

3. Once I have completed all the business as usual deliverables associated with my role – these are the things that my boss will hold me accountable for – for the balance of my workday I can plan for and work on deliverables that are coming up in the next week, month or quarter, invest in personal development and also research.

4. I'm agile to respond to any urgent and unplanned deliverables that occur – or work with and assist others who may need an extra hand.

5. Most importantly for me, I have created the opportunity of **time** captured as a **profit**. By getting my accountable deliverables completed, I have availed myself of the opportunity to be involved with or learn something new should the opportunity arise – *because I can*.

My battle rhythm strategies

1. If you don't need to compete – don't compete. Identify where your time is best spent – and focus your attention there. Choose your response.

2. Work to create and profit from the time you can capture by working with focused efficiency.

3. Plan to identify the work that you are required to deliver on in your immediate and forecast future.

4. Be available to respond to any urgent and unplanned work as it creates as-yet-unrecognised opportunities in the future.

5. Always share your time generously when requested. Always share your knowledge and experience generously when solicited. Recognise that unsolicited advice is rarely appreciated.

To close out this chapter, I recognise that whilst I have provided to you an overview of what a battle rhythm is, and introduced to you the discipline I apply into my work practices that reflect a battle rhythm – you are still left wanting and perhaps curious as to the business as usual practices that I have developed and successfully applied to get the work that I am held accountable for completed in the opening hours of my business day.

Once again, I remind you that *I did not even realise this outcome existed until the end*. Be patient and try to enjoy the read.

To mollify, let us take a moment to reflect on some of the things you may have learnt in this chapter:

1. New opportunities exist if you choose to identify challenge and opportunities instead of nuisance and adversity.

2. Where some see an opportunity for a competitive edge others see redundancy.

3. We can all enjoy restful slumber and enjoy a fruitful work-life balance if we turn the Zeigarnik Effect – *where people remember uncomplete or interrupted tasks better than completed tasks* – to our advantage.

4. If you don't need to compete – don't compete. Identify where your time is best spent – and focus your attention there. Choose your response.

5. During the period of 544–496 BCE in ancient China lived a revered and successful Taoist general, military strategist and philosopher Sun Tzu, whose visionary leadership and discipline still resonates as strongly in contemporary times, as his legend prevailed in history.

> *"New opportunities exist if you choose to identify challenge and opportunities instead of nuisance and adversity."*
>
> **Katrina Wilson**

CHAPTER 4

Elevator Pitch

The following chapters of this book are not written as filler. These experiences and observations captured are the reason that I started to develop RUGBY Quality Review in the first place. I captured them because I saw some of the same decision points, behaviours, conflicts and failures occur in other workplaces – which makes them standard and not unique.

You may be curious as to what the RUGBY Quality Review process is, and how it could be deployed across your business or workplace – it is however, important that if you do skip through the following chapters, that you do return to them.

These observations and experiences are important to evidence that RUGBY Quality Review is an innovative business process that provides to employees a visual cue that requires attention and response.

These chapters provide credibility and examples that will support you, as you apply RUGBY Mindset and Quality Review practically yourself and across your business, because you too may identify some of these decision points, behaviours, conflicts and failures within your own workplace.

By reading these chapters, you will realise that you are not alone in your business challenges, as others share your experiences and pain. You will also provide yourself with a unique opportunity towards developing a business vernacular that will support you as you respond to the quality business practices your business needs, *not to survive but to thrive.*

The potential for RUGBY Mindset and Quality Review is best shared in capturing the conversation or elevator pitch I had with the expensive (but well worth the investment) lawyer who I consulted with to assess the suitability and potential of success in applying for the intellectual property for RUGBY Mindset and Quality Review.

I knew before attending that meeting that the conversation that I was just about to have was going to be costly, because the hourly rate charged by a legal specialist would far surpass my own modest earnings. So to ensure that my hard earned dollar was well spent I prepared for our meeting.

I prepared by downloading from his business website commercial information related to the services of the firm, and it was from this that our conversation developed. Of course, our conversation opened with the extension of social pleasantries that all meetings mature from, what follows is our dialogue immediately following our five minutes invested in polite conversation and social pleasantries.

"Before I came to meet with you today, I downloaded from your website some commercial information related to the services that your firm specialises in. By looking at this document, can you:

- be confident that the information that it contains is current, correct and appropriately captures the services of your firm?

- assure your staff, that the information that it contains captures the current and correct best practice, discipline and services of your business?

- tell me the last time that this document, and further the website I downloaded it from was last reviewed and/or updated?

- know that all relevant stakeholders within your firm have contributed to and been informed of the information and practices that they will be held accountable and responsible for in their role with your firm?"

His response to these questions was at first a blank look and then an offering. "Well, I can't answer immediately... but I could go out the back to the office and probably find out."

There is no shame in admitting that my heart skipped a beat, not only because I realised I had pitched the right questions and had probably asked questions that he had never had raised before, but because I had piqued his interest and asked questions he had no confident answer for. So, I closed with one final statement and one final question.

"Recognising that accreditation and recognition of Quality Assurance with external certification bodies is largely dependent upon evidencing how a business practices what they have been certified for:

- How confident are you, as the managing partner of this firm, that the practices and procedures that your firm has documented as part of your business and quality management practices and compliance are not only used, but reviewed regularly and updated as something important or critical changes in your business?"

You see where I am going here don't you? The conversation did not close, the conversation matured. The conversation matured as the clock ticked, as the clocked ticked, I was spending money. So I offered my 'what if's':

- "What if I was to share with you, that I have developed a quality review and business process, from which if you were asked that question in the future, you would be able to immediately respond with 'that document, process or procedure was reviewed in the last one month, three months, six months or 12 months'?"

- "What if I was to further offer that by using this business and quality review process it would take the pressure off you and your staff when your business was undergoing an external independent audit?"

- "What if I said that this process would give you confidence that your business was being administered optimally with risk considered, by providing to the people working for you, a visual cue to pause and credibly review the information that they were working from?"

My lawyers response? "I would be interested in that."

My conversation with the lawyer that day was the first time I had shared the concept of RUGBY Quality Review and my first audience. Had the lawyer not shown any interest or curiosity towards what I was bringing to the table – I would not have spent the time and money in applying to secure its intellectual property.

So what did I bring to the table that day?

RUGBY Quality Review has been developed to:

- Cradle a competitive edge in business. It has been *developed from* a successful site safety practice and *transformed towards* a competitive business edge through quality business practices.

- Capitalise on a person's natural response and ability to respond to visual cues – and apply it practically by crafting a business pause to recognise and respond to fatigued or redundant business practices.

- Transform the perception of quality in business from an 'ugly baby', by recognising that just as a baby that receives attention is nurtured and loved is never 'ugly', quality business and assurance practices that receive attention, are nurtured and loved are never 'ugly'.

- Focus attention on, nurturing and loving an auditable business requirement that most businesses stumble to maintain, and recognise that quality is never only *one* person's job – it's *every* person's job.

- Provide an opportunity for a business to evidence and support their auditing and compliance certification requirements, and promote best practice and the opportunity to capture and respond to change, or a significant commercial change, or shift in your business – translating to profit.

What my lawyer showed most interest in though is that a business does not need to employ additional resources, purchase sophisticated software or licences or attend training to implement RUGBY Quality Review.

A business need only purchase this book and access the talent and resources they currently employ to implement RUGBY Quality Review as a business as usual practice by practically applying a battle rhythm, an ARCI matrix and visual cues.

> *"RUGBY Quality Review is an innovative business process that provides employers and employees with a visual cue to provoke a required business response."*
>
> **Katrina Wilson**

SECTION 2

Forming

CHAPTER 5

Concept of RUGBY Quality Review

Step 1: Identify Time

Identify the time that your business has to review its quality practices and documentation. For example:

- Business Trading Days: Monday – Friday = five days per week

- Business Trading Hours: 0800 – 1700 = 40 hours per week

Step 2: Establish a battle rhythm to capture the operational cadence of your business.

- Identify the days that your business does not operate (i.e. Weekends; Public Holidays; Planned Shutdown Periods).

Public Holidays in Queensland (2017)		Planned Shutdown Periods
02 January 2017	New Year's Day	03 – 07 January 2017
26 January 2017	Australia Day	
14 April 2017	Good Friday	
17 April 2017	Easter Monday	
25 April 2017	Anzac Day	
01 May 2017	Labour Day	
16 August 2017	Royal Brisbane Show	
02 October 2017	Queen's Birthday	
25 December 2017	Christmas Day	27 – 30 December 2017
26 December 2017	Boxing Day	

- Nuance your operational calendar by anticipating potential leave. For example, if a public holiday falls close to a weekend, you or your employees may take the opportunity of leave from the office to enjoy an even longer weekend.

Public Holidays in Queensland (2017)		Anticipated Leave
02 January 2017	New Year's Day	09 – 14 January 2017
26 January 2017	Australia Day	27 January 2017
14 April 2017	Good Friday	18 – 22 April 2017
17 April 2017	Easter Monday	
25 April 2017	Anzac Day	24 April – 02 May 2017
01 May 2017	Labour Day	
16 August 2017	Royal Brisbane Show	17 – 19 August 2017
02 October 2017	Queen's Birthday	29 September 2017
25 December 2017	Christmas Day	
26 December 2017	Boxing Day	

Step 3: Capture visually the operational cadence of your business

Capture the Public Holidays, planned shutdowns of your business and the anticipated leave in one visual capture.

2017 calendar showing all twelve months with legend: Gazetted Public Holiday 2017, Planned Shutdown Periods, Anticipated Leave.

Step 4: RUGBY Review Cadence

Establish a battle rhythm or operational cadence to identify the best time your business has available to review critical information and documentation that suits your business high and low activity periods.

Below is an example of a RUGBY Battle Rhythm. This is an example of how you can begin to capture the optimal periods in your business by identifying the days that your business will operate.

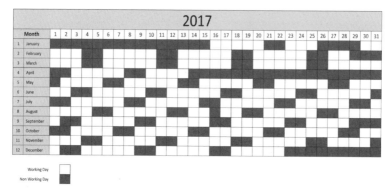

Identify visually the peak and optimal review periods of your business and design a RUGBY Review Cadence to suit your business.

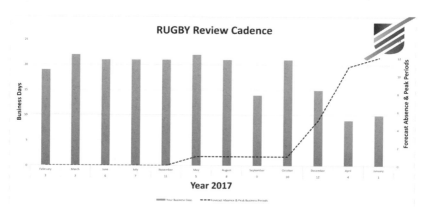

This graph is a visual capture of the review cadence (above). It captures:

- The number of business days your business will operate in each month.

- The forecast absences, which includes gazetted public holidays and the anticipated leave you have forecast.

From this graph you can identify:

- The peak periods of your business, when staffing may be low or activity may be high – you **should not** plan any significant quality reviews in this period.

  - *January, April and December 2017.*

- The optimal periods of your business, when staffing is at capacity and activity may be low – you **should** plan your quality reviews in this period.

  - *February, March, May, June, July, August, September, October, November 2017.*

Step 5: RUGBY Quality Review Battle Rhythm

Design a RUGBY Quality Review Battle Rhythm to suit your business by isolating the peak periods of your business and assigning a review indicator against the optimal periods of your business.

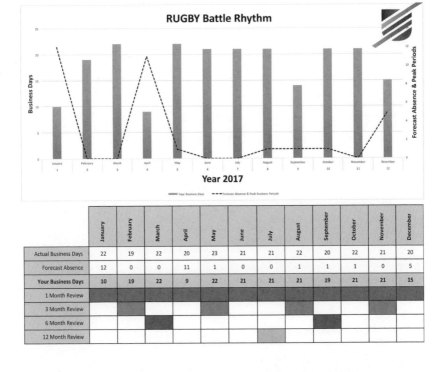

	January	February	March	April	May	June	July	August	September	October	November	December
Actual Business Days	22	19	22	20	23	21	21	22	20	22	21	20
Forecast Absence	12	0	0	11	1	0	0	1	1	1	0	5
Your Business Days	10	19	22	9	22	21	21	21	19	21	21	15
1 Month Review												
3 Month Review												
6 Month Review												
12 Month Review												

Step 6: RUGBY Review Protocols

Assign review protocols that suit your business needs to communicate to your employees the framework, understanding, expectation and standard that your business has set to support its focus towards total quality review and management, and continual improvement.

Tag Identifier	Review Cadence	Priority / Focus	Protocols
Red	Every 1 month	High	Documentation and information that: • Requires vigilance and critical review – e.g. commercial, legal or risk. • References or is dependent on information maintained or compliant to an external source or body (such as ISO compliance etc). • Contains information that is constantly changing. • Contains hyperlinks and website url threads.
Green	Every 3 months	High to Medium	Documentation and information that: • Requires quarterly critical review for accuracy, relevance and compliance.
Blue	Every 6 months	Medium	Documentation and information that: • Requires periodic review for accuracy, relevance and compliance.
Yellow	Every 12 months	Medium to Low	Documentation and information that: • Requires once yearly review for accuracy, relevance and compliance.

Step 7: RUGBY Promotion, Maintenance and Demotion Protocols

This is the most important review stage of RUGBY Quality Review because it highlights the fact that nothing remains stagnant in business – only one thing needs to change for everything to change.

Something that *is not considered* critical in your business right now may be critical to your business *in the future*. Equally, something that *is considered* critical in your business right now, may not be critical to your business *in the future*.

To mitigate dormancy, identify the protocols that your business will use to promote, maintain or demote documentation and information for review.

Current Tag Identifier	Promote	Maintain	Demote
	Documentation has not required any significant change or update.	Documentation has required update.	Documentation has required significant changes.
Red	Green	Red	Red
Green	Blue	Green	Red
Blue	Yellow	Blue	Green
Yellow	Yellow	Yellow	Blue

Step 8: RUGBY Identifiers

Place a visual cue on all documentation, online references or webpages that your business uses, produces, references or promotes.

Red	Green	Blue	Yellow
Every 1 Month	Every 3 Months	Every 6 Months	Every 12 Months

Step 9: RUGBY Responsibilities

Capture who is required to contribute in critically reviewing and updating your business documentation logically and identify the position from which they will contribute.

Contributors	Responsibilities	Description
Responsible	**A**ccountable	Identify the people who will be held **accountable** for the review.
Governing	**R**esponsible	Identify people who will manage and be held **responsible** for the review.
Benefactor	**C**ontribute	Identify the people who **contribute** to and should be consulted to ensure the information is consistent across the business.
Your Employees	**I**nformed	Identify the people who should be considered and **informed** to ensure the information that they are working with is current.

Step 10: RUGBY Behaviours

	Behaviour	Definition
Reinvigorate	**Reinvigorate** your existing quality assurance model and practices.	**Reinvigorate** 1. Give new energy or strength to something.
Galvanise	**Galvanise** and support your talent to contribute towards your quality assurance business model.	**Galvanise** 1. Shock or excite (someone) into taking action. 2. A person or a group of people having such ability.
Beneficiate	**Beneficiate** your quality management fundamentals to effectively deliver on your continual improvement and compliance agenda.	**Beneficiate** 1. To treat a raw material to improve its properties. 2. To subject to a process or treatment, with the aim of readying for some purpose, improvement or to remedy a condition.
You	**You** are accountable to respond to the challenges in your business or your role by focusing your *talent* of skill where it is required.	**Talent** 1. Natural endowment or ability of a superior quality. 2. A person or a group of people having such ability.

Final Step: Capture the Time Your Business has to Review and Improve Quality

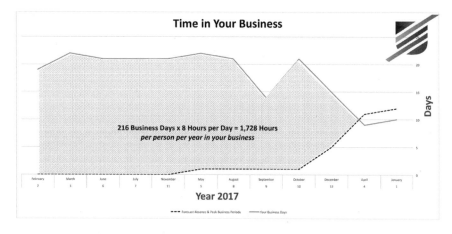

CHAPTER 6

The Game of Rugby

> *"A RUGBY Mindset starts by recognising that the team who wins the game, wins, not because of their application and execution of a superior playbook or talent – they win because they made the fewest number of mistakes."*
>
> Katrina Wilson

Here is what I **know** about the game of rugby.

- Rugby identifies as one of Australia and New Zealand's national sports and its contributors or players form as a team.

- At any one time, the game is played by two opposing teams.

- The sport is structured by recognition and adherence to a set of rules.

- Adherence to the rules of the game are monitored and imposed by two referees, two touch judges, a video referee and a timekeeper (rugby league). That counts as six people who are accountable for how evenly or fairly this game is regulated – *how level the playing field is.*

- If any one person on a team doesn't adhere to, or inadvertently contravenes the rules of the game, a penalty is *bestowed against* the team whose player transgressed, which then translates as a penalty *awarded to* their opposition.

It is the carrot and stick scenario, with a twist – if you breach the rules you end up with a lose–lose result. If you don't adhere to the rules of the game *your team* gets hit with the stick and *your opposition* gets the carrot. *You take a hit and you are left without a reward.*

- The sport is executed or delivered by a number of players (the team) who are strategically placed into positions that work to their strengths.

- Each team strengthens their potential for success through agility and redundancy.

  Redundancy in the true definition of the word and represented by the additional players, who are skilled and available to contribute as required, should fatigue or injury occur during the game. *You might not need to use them, but you have them available should you need them for the state of play to either change or continue.*

- The success or failure of rugby's ultimate objective – which is to win the game – is in having the best people, making the best decisions, at the best time applied with the best focus and effort. This is why it is called a 'team'.

- The challenge of the game is that the opposing team has the same resources, objectives and focus.

- The game outcome hinges in how each team's talent is focused and deployed as the game is in play, with the supremacy of a team reflected in how they progress as leaders throughout the season and ultimately recognised as the superior team of the season.

Rugby in Australia and New Zealand is a national sport but the discipline and adherence to the rules assigned to a sport are just as applicable to Gridiron, Basketball, Baseball, Football, Soccer, Lacrosse, Polo, Ice Hockey, Netball, Dragon Boat Racing, Chess or Quidditch – as the discipline, focus and objective is the same.

Using rugby as an analogy – it is an activity that:

- People get passionate about.

- Gets people active and engaged.

- Promotes a shared common interest.

What I appreciate the most about rugby the game, is that it is an activity that starts conversations, transcends sex, race, creed or preference, and it is a sport that unifies local, national and global communities.

Here is what I **don't** know about the game of rugby.

- The rules.

I have never played the game, so I've never learned the rules. If I haven't played – then I haven't contributed. What this means is that until I learn and understand the rules of the game, I will *never* be in a position to credibly contribute or offer an opinion towards any decision that is made when I perceive a rule transgression.

To a true rugby enthusiast, I'm an apathetic bystander. I don't experience the euphoric highs when a team wins and I don't experience the despair of the downtrodden when a team loses.

My disposition and behaviour doesn't change upon the outcome of a game – it is not an outcome I place any value against therefore I am unmoved. Bystander apathy and, by extension, a person who is identified as an apathetic bystander – has at its very core, a human attempt at self-preservation – a conscious decision *to not be involved* in something that has the potential to disrupt our personal equilibrium, challenge our values or impact on our situation in life.

Which is why I rarely watch a game on television. I think I would prefer to purposefully slam my hand in a car door than endure watching a game of rugby on television – which flies in the face of any genetic predisposition or coding, because with the exception of my beautiful mother, everyone else in my direct family tree are keen on the sport. Thinking about it – it could be a learned behaviour from my mum…

I'm an apathetic bystander when I don't watch the game on television, because I don't understand the play by play, even as the commentators break it down, and I don't care about the outcome.

You may however, find me in the grandstand – cheering on my chosen team because I love the atmosphere. Most likely, you will find me at an Australia / New Zealand game, not only to in a small way, participate in the friendly antipodean rugby rivalry between our two countries – but also to see those hulking New Zealand boys perform the Haka. Scares me every time!

You might find me in a grandstand because whilst I don't understand the rules of the game or the play by play, I do have a frame of reference. I recognise, understand and appreciate the divided response revealed across the stadium as the game is in play and I recognise that each response voiced by each team's supporters, is dependent on the success made by or failure called against the team they support.

On the rare occasion that you find me in a grandstand, I am there because I **do** care about the outcome of the game, I **am** enjoying and participating in the atmosphere and I most certainly **am not** an apathetic bystander – *I am there because I choose to be there.*

One final thought on the game of rugby: When the teams and state of play are *evenly matched in skill and resources*, the team who wins the game, wins, *not* because of their application and execution of a superior playbook or talent – they win because they made the *fewest* mistakes.

This is where a RUGBY Mindset starts – by recognising that in business and in life, mistakes are going to occur because we are mere mortals who:

- Make mistakes and err in our judgements. Every country and culture across the world has a judicial system in place for this very reason.

- Have potential, when supported within a healthy environment, to learn from our mistakes.

- Share in good faith and as part of our generous nature, our failures transparently, so that others may benefit and cast a thought to *our* experiences before they potentially make the same mistakes.

- Embrace opportunities and make decisions, to not only mitigate *but eliminate* the potential for the same mistake to occur again, thereby not leaving ourselves unnecessarily vulnerable.

A RUGBY Mindset promotes recognition that:

- A perfect world – a world with no mistakes in it – does not exist.

- Your competitive edge is assured if you can structure your business and business practices to make the *fewest* mistakes.

- A little effort and focus can transform the tarnished coin of failure into the polished currency of an enhanced competitive edge and profit for yourself, your employer and business.

Be proactive in your business disciplines to recognise and capture change when it occurs and mitigate the potential for eventual loss or failure by acting on it.

Benefit and be comforted by the fact that the evolution of our species occurred because of our ability to respond and adapt.

> *"A little effort and focus can transform the tarnished coin of failure into the polished currency of an enhanced competitive edge and profit for yourself, your employer and business."*
>
> **Katrina Wilson**

CHAPTER 7

A RUGBY Mindset

Does a parallel exist between rugby the sport and business? I think it does and what follows is the foundation of a RUGBY Mindset.

There is no 'I' in TEAM

Success occurs, when a disciplined focus is applied, by a number of people, who contribute and concentrate their effort effectively towards delivering on an identified outcome – success.

Whether you are a one-person business or an employee of a business or organisation, there will always exist a number of people you will work with to deliver on your service or role.

A business will always have as considerations, their clients, their suppliers, their consultants, their supply chain, their peers, colleagues, employees and competitors.

Those who make the fewest mistakes wins

Success is weighted towards the team or business who make fewer mistakes than their competitor does.

Influence your potential to succeed through innovation

Success hinges on a team's or business's ability to successfully identify redundancy and apply it as innovation throughout the game or their business.

I mentioned in an earlier chapter that within the sport redundancy is evident through additional players, who are skilled and available to contribute as required, should fatigue or injury occur during the game.

You might not need to use them, but you have them on the sidelines should you need them for the game to either change or continue.

Business redundancy *to people* has fear associated to it. However, it does not need to – nor should it – because redundancy in business should reflect correctly identifying workplace practices or contributions that no longer supports a business to succeed.

Business redundancy does not mean that a person should no longer have a job because the role that they are currently employed to, no longer serves the success of the business. *Their skills could be used in other areas of a business.*

It does mean that a business should look to improve efficiencies and eliminate the workplace practices and contributions that no longer supports its success. It makes no sense to continue to overlook a stressed or fatigued business model just because 'that's the way we have always done it'.

Regardless, *people* mostly identify redundancy in business with poor business performance, which reflects as financial loss and potentially someone losing their job or business.

I strongly recommend to you now, the identification of potential for redundancy in your business should be captured as innovation *not redundancy* – and I do this because a *person's* understanding of redundancy in a game of rugby, which is to have capacity to change and/or continue the game, is in direct contradiction to their association of redundancy in business.

Existing out there in our business world today are two or three generations of employees, many of whom associate the word redundancy with a negative event.

If you want your employees to start being committed, positive and innovative in their business approach to profit from identifying redundancy – don't use the word redundancy – use the word innovation. You will enjoy a different energy in your workplace or business and you will enjoy a different conversation.

One final thought – why do people lose colour and break out in a sweat when the word redundancy is used? This is not an exaggeration, I have seen this response – it is almost like a dirty word or rules one to three of *Fight Club*:

> "The first rule of Fight Club is: You do not talk about Fight Club. The second rule of Fight Club is: You do not talk about Fight Club. Third rule of Fight Club: Someone yells stop, goes limp, taps out, the fight is over."

Their response is because it's the outcome that they have been exposed to when a business fails to recognise, capture and respond to change early.

For a business to determine its agility and move towards supremacy – it requires intermediation of human agency, geared towards creating an opportunity to succeed or profit, by responding to necessary change through innovation.

Competitive edge – what changes the game?

Success translates as a competitive edge when a team or business seeks to not only identify but also respond to change, as it occurs, to strengthen their play or business through innovation.

RUGBY Quality Review has been developed to cradle competitive edge in business and quality practices. It has been *developed from* a successful site safety practice and *transformed towards* a competitive edge through an innovative approach to quality business practices.

A competitive edge can be resolute in your business by introducing RUGBY Quality Review as a *business as usual practice*, because I can find no indication that any other business captures or responds to quality assurance and compliance in this way. Right now, it is unique, and if you start using it – you create the opportunity of creating for your business – a competitive edge.

Forming, storming, norming and performing

A team or business's future success lies in the way that they form, storm, norm and perform.

The game of rugby captures visually the way that a team forms, storms, norms and performs.

The first half of a rugby game is where it forms, and it is usually fierce and fast-paced – with each team's players demonstrating their perceived dominance for the benefit of the other team – *not the spectators*. This is a display of strength and agility, which influences the decisions that the players make in how they execute *their* game.

It is in the first half of a game when the most conflicts and physical tussles occur. When the pressure is off – and the testosterone is abundant. A true rugby enthusiast could decry this statement – and I would concede to their superior knowledge and passion – nevertheless, it is my observation.

By the second half of the game, you see the players transitioning from *form* into *storm*, where they are applying more strategy into their play. It is in the second half of a game where you will see a team communicating more volubly across the field, as they seek to establish a competitive edge in the game and it is in this time that you will see redundancy employed through the change-out of players.

It is leading into the closing minutes of the game that you see the number of mistakes increase. This is the busiest time for the adjudicators of the game and it is where the most pressure is applied. Because this is a finite period, the game ends with the final siren. One team wins and another loses.

So where does a rugby team norm? They norm in the midpoint of the game, at half time, when they huddle with their coach, which gives them the opportunity to review the first half and make changes to their line-up or playbook.

They norm in the dressing room after the game as they start to mentally review their internal play by play of the game and their contribution towards it.

They norm in the post-game briefing with their team and coach. They norm as they review the game onscreen and they norm as they look to improve their physical conditioning towards optimal efficiency – when they hit the weight benches, find themselves with a bunch of balls standing in front of a goal post or passing a ball across the field.

When a player does this, they are self-regulating. They are moving from *norm* into *perform*, they are looking to identify what they did well, they are looking to identify what they did not do well, and they are looking to improve.

Player's norm so they can contribute to the best of their ability as they *perform*; for themselves, for their team and for their employer – the people who help them put bread and butter on their table.

It is the same in business. How a business forms and storms, how they align their employee base and execute their business is unique to them – and has no relevance to RUGBY Quality Review.

RUGBY Quality Review has been developed to fit into the norming stage of business. It has been structured so that it can be easily embraced and adopted within a business as a business as usual practice. Yes, it is an innovative approach to quality management and review, because it is fresh – *but there is nothing spectacular about it, until a person or business starts using it to gain a competitive edge and evidence its profit.*

RUGBY Quality Review forms, storms, norms and performs by:

- **Forming** with a shared focus. Employees will establish and recognise accountabilities, responsibilities, contributions and behaviours that align with the businesses values and focus.

- **Storming** with respect. Employees demonstrate a collaborative focus towards a shared outcome; and share equally the responsibilities of success and failure.

- **Norming** with integrity and competence. Employees will recognise that their contribution towards quality review and continual improvement in the workplace significantly influences the concept of quality attributed to the business.

- **Performing** with a shared focus.

> *"The norming stage of business is the quiet, potentially reflective period, where the pressure is less and time seems abundant, and it is this time that is captured by a battle rhythm."*
>
> **Katrina Wilson**

CHAPTER 8

Your Organisational Culture

What makes us feel good about work? Some may say that we feel better and more engaged in the work that we do, if we know we are working towards something, if our output is measurable and our effort is acknowledged.

If you form to implement RUGBY Quality Review into your business, your interest will be best served if you recognise that, as you can see from the earlier chapter, the quality review process itself is a very easy process to implement. But any effort you make will be derailed if you don't have an organisational culture that is focused on quality – and it needs to start from the top down.

If the owner of a business, or if the most senior executive of a business, does not place value on quality – then the people in the subordinate positions that follow are not going to place any value on it either. The apple doesn't fall far from the tree. For too many years, the tail has wagged that 'underdog' quality. I'm thinking that it might just be time for that 'underdog' quality to start wagging the tail.

An undocumented event in Isaac Newtons life..........

> *"If the owner of a business or most senior executive of a business does not place value on quality – then the people in the subordinate positions that follow are not going to place any value on it either."*
>
> **Katrina Wilson**

CHAPTER 9

Where it all Began

For the first part of 2015 I was unemployed and seemingly unemployable in a market flooded with candidates. At the time, I thought it was the very worst of luck, and that I had made some very poor career decisions which had left me vulnerable.

I reassured myself that I deserved a break; after all, in the five years before this forced sojourn, I had undertaken a number of contract roles within the major projects and construction industries both in Australia and overseas in South Korea – bouncing from one to another.

I fortified myself by choosing to see my unemployed status as the opportunity of an unplanned holiday, but, as my unemployment turned from weeks into months, I saw the financial savings I had made through hard work, personal discipline and the sacrifice of fabulous holidays dwindling at an alarming rate, and I was concerned. Very concerned, because I did not know how long I would have to wait before I enjoyed the benefit of a regular income again.

As anybody who has experienced unemployment will tell you, there are many hours to fill in your day, even after you have trawled through the newly advertised positions vacant on the online job boards, submitted your applications and trod the path between recruitment offices. I realised that I would need to apply myself towards personal employment if I was to use this time advantageously – and to spend some time in identifying my point of difference – what would identify me as unique to everyone else.

It was in this time, it was in that space that I developed RUGBY Quality Review and started to give some thought towards the business mindset it would need to support it – *because I had time to think, I had time to interrogate, I had time to challenge and most importantly – **I had time to be creative**.*

Therefore, my unemployment status in early 2015 ended up being the break that I needed in the end – because it provided to me the opportunity to reflect upon the mistakes that litter my work history and to turn it around towards capturing something positive.

This book and RUGBY Mindset and Quality Review are the result.

> *"When you have time to think, you create the opportunity to interrogate what you know and you have time to be creative."*
>
> **Katrina Wilson**

CHAPTER 10

Dugald River

Whilst working out at Dugald River, I had the opportunity to interview and feature in the MMG company magazine *Horizon* to share a little of what it was like to work out there on site.

Below is what I had to say at the time – and it's still true today – I smile every time I think of my time spent on site, the experiences that I had and the fabulous people I worked with.

Feature Article – MMG Horizon (Issue 15 | June 2013)

I've worked on the Dugald River project for nearly two years now. I started off working for one of the contractors involved in the project, and then had the opportunity to join MMG in a site-based role in October last year.

Whilst always eager for new experiences, when I was given the opportunity to work at site I was unsure of how I would embrace this new challenge. Certainly my family and friends were unsure of my transition from high heels and city living, to hard hats and 6.00 am pre-start meetings.

In terms of the skills required for the role I was comfortable, but I'd never worked on a site before, never been so far west, and I was relocating to an isolated environment where I did not have the comfort of a familiar face. Happily, there was no need to worry – within a couple of days of arriving at site I felt like I'd been here for a month.

What we are doing here on site is truly amazing – to be at the start-up of a project is exceptional. The strong leadership and professional integrity demonstrated every day by the MMG management team I work with is inspiring, and essential when working in a robust and challenging environment.

The project is unique in that there are simultaneous operations between the construction and mining effort. What that means is that we have a 'One Team' focus. In the time I've been on site I have seen significant and visible changes. Traffic management has been a big focus area as we put rigour around how the site interacts, for example the coordination between the mining activity, bulk earthworks, crushing and screening and the construction of the mine permanent village which is conducted by contractors on site.

Strong communication across the site is vital for project and operational effectiveness, and for safety. Important changes and information are planned for and communicated via site bulletins. Each of these are signed off by management from Operations and Construction, and then communicated site wide – which demonstrates MMG's core values of safety, integrity, action and results.

Each day kicks off with a pre-start meeting. Walking from the fly camp to the MMG site office is one of my favourite times of day – it's always fresh and it always takes my breath away. There's harmony in seeing the high visibility tape on our PPE slowly emerge in the dawn light as we progress to our daily pre-start meetings.

Our daily pre-start meetings are 15 minutes for our team to identify and highlight the successes we delivered the previous day and to focus on the works that are scheduled to be conducted that day. It's an opportunity for us to all draw together, share information and set the focus for the day.

Throughout the day I work closely with the construction management team – we manage the day to day construction effort and the contractors on site.

One of the things that can be commended is the investment in technology and infrastructure at Dugald River. As a matter of fact, the mobile technology signal strength we enjoy here at Dugald River is stronger than the signal strength our closest neighbours in Cloncurry and Mount Isa enjoy. At the business end of things, the virtual environment that has been provided here at site ensures that meetings are interactive and conducted in real time, meaning meetings and workflow between site and Group Office are seamless.

It's not all hard work. At the close of each day we have camp facilities that we take full advantage of. There's a gym here and quite a few of the team have a really healthy focus. The food we eat here on site is really healthy too. We also have a social club, and often they hold events like 'Jag the Joker', 'Trivia Nights', movie nights on the deck, or as we call them 'Deck Chair Premier' nights, and of course, being proudly located in Queensland, we host an eventful 'State of Origin'.

The majority of us within construction work a three week on, one week off roster. I love that; I work hard for three weeks and then get a week off – every single month – 12 weeks holiday a year.

But what I love the most about working on this project, and out at site, is the strength of our team. There is a very respectful culture; respectful of the environment and respectful of each other. I truly feel I have found my niche here at Dugald River. Sure, there are challenges where you really just have to laugh or cry, but I haven't cried yet.

As the project moves from a construction focus to an operational focus over the coming two years, there will be more of a need for people to come and work here at site. I really encourage people to consider it; it's a fantastic opportunity to work with a respectful, welcoming team.

FEATURES

LIFE AT... DUGALD RIVER

By Katrina Wilson, Senior Site Administrator, Dugald River

I've worked on the Dugald River project for nearly two years now. I started off working for one of the contractors involved in the project, and then had the opportunity to join MMG in a site-based role in October last year.

Image: Senior Site Administrator at Dugald River Katrina Wilson.

Whilst always eager for new experiences, when I was given the opportunity to work at site I was unsure of how I would embrace this new challenge. Certainly my family and friends were unsure of my transition from high heels and city living, to hard hats and 6.00am pre-start meetings.

In terms of the skills required for the role I was comfortable, but I'd never worked on a site before, never been so far west, and I was relocating to an isolated environment where I did not have the comfort of a familiar face. Happily, there was no need to worry – within a couple of days of arriving at site, I felt like I'd been here for a month.

What we are doing here on site is truly amazing – to be at the start-up of a project is exceptional. The strong leadership and professional integrity demonstrated every day by the MMG management team I work with is inspiring, and essential when working in a robust and challenging environment.

The project is unique in that there are simultaneous operations between the construction and mining effort. What that means is that we have a 'One Team' focus. In the time I've been on site I have seen significant and visible changes. Traffic management has been a big focus area as we put rigour around how the site interacts, for example the coordination between the mining activity, bulk earthworks, crushing and screening and the construction of the mine permanent village which is conducted by contractors on site.

Strong communication across the site is vital for project and operational effectiveness, and for safety. Important changes and information are planned for and communicated via site bulletins. Each of these are signed off by management from Operations and Construction, and then communicated site wide – which demonstrates MMG's core values of safety, integrity, action and results.

Each day kicks off with a pre-start meeting. Walking from the fly camp to the MMG site office is one of my favourite times of day – it's always fresh and it always takes my breath away. There's a harmony in seeing the high visibility tape on our PPE slowly emerge in the dawn light as we progress to our daily pre-start meetings.

Image: The day at Dugald River starts with a spectacular sunrise... and finishes just as majestically. Photos taken by Dugald River site administrator Sanja Mladjenovic.

Our daily pre-start meetings are 15 minutes for our team to identify and highlight the successes we delivered the previous day and to focus on the works that are scheduled to be conducted that day. It's an opportunity for us to all draw together, share information and set the focus for the day.

Throughout the day I work closely with the construction management team – we manage the day to day construction effort and the contractors on site.

One of the things that can be commended is the investment in technology and infrastructure at Dugald River. As a matter of fact, the mobile technology signal strength we enjoy here at Dugald River is stronger than the signal strength our closest neighbours at Cloncurry and Mount Isa enjoy. At the business end of things, the virtual environment that has been provided here at site ensures that meetings are interactive and conducted in real time, meaning meetings and workflow between site and Group Office are seamless.

It's not all hard work. At the close of each day we have camp facilities that we take full advantage of. There's a gym here and quite a few of the team have a really healthy focus. The food we eat here on site is really healthy too. We also have a social club, and often they hold events like 'Jag the Joker', 'Trivia Nights', movie nights on the deck, or as we call them, 'Deck Chair Premier' nights, and of course, being proudly located in Queensland, we host an eventful 'State of Origin'.

The majority of us within construction work a three week on, one week off roster. I love that; I work hard for three weeks and then get a week off – every single month – 12 weeks holiday a year.

But what I love most about working on this project, and out at site, is the strength of the team. There is a very respectful culture; respectful of the environment and respectful of each other. I truly feel I have found my niche here at Dugald River. Sure, there are challenges where you really just have to laugh or cry, but I haven't cried yet.

As the project moves from a construction focus to an operational focus over the coming two years, there will be more of a need for people to come and work here at site. I really encourage people to consider it; it's a fantastic opportunity to work with a respectful, welcoming team.

The Dugald River construction project was greenfield, which means that the project was being developed and constructed on land that had never been developed to mine and extract ore. The project scope, while I was working on it, was in developing and drilling underground for ore and constructing a processing plant, accommodation village, site access and air strip. It was a 'fresh' project and it was executed and delivered under simultaneous operations or 'SIMOPS' as it was known on site, between Mine Operations (drilling and extracting the ore) and Civil Construction works – and it was very exciting!

The leadership demonstrated by the Site Executive and Construction Site Managers were inspiring with their collaboration and focus. These men worked together to ensure that the project was delivered, safely, with consideration, compliance, on time and within the scope, schedule and budget – which incidentally is the focus that all successful projects lead with.

For a person who has a curious nature, this project was an excellent launchpad for my new career path. Not only had I never worked on a construction project before, I had never worked on a billion-dollar project before, nor had I ever worked in such an isolated location.

For a city girl from Brisbane, this was a big step towards developing my skillset and working on my personal and professional growth. I was terrified at what I was committing to and contributing towards – but I did it anyway.

Working at an isolated and remote location in Australia, on a busy construction site, was at first intimidating in its unfamiliarity – it is a tough terrain and environment, which goes hand in hand with the people who work in these environments. My peers on site were some of the most mentally tough and resilient people I have ever met. We get mentally tough because we need to – to survive the harsh realities of the site's remoteness and the high-risk work that we do.

Contrary to what I said at the time of interviewing for the magazine article – I recall that there were a couple of occasions that my tears mixed with my shampoo at the end of a workday.

In contrast and perhaps to provide some balance, the work and site activities were interesting. The cost of a few wasted tears was worth the amazing opportunity I had working on site.

I had transitioned from a 9–5 workweek to a Fly-In Fly-Out (FIFO) employee on a project that brought together many interesting people from all over Australia, with strengths and capabilities, experience and a work history that brought the project from concept to life.

My father raised my brothers, sisters and I with the adage "You were born with two ears, two eyes and one mouth. Use them in that order." It's sound advice you can appreciate as an adult – but as a child, it's not something that you want to hear.

It is one of the behaviours that I model to this day – I listen, I watch and I learn.

On site at Dugald River – being such an unfamiliar experience – to be situationally aware of my environment I listened to, and watched, what my colleagues did that were successful. Most importantly, I made sure that I listened to and watched what my colleagues did on site that was not successful – no point in more than one of us making the same mistake!

The concept of the RUGBY Quality and Review system for business came to life in early 2015 as I recalled all the things that I had learnt from my experiences on site at Dugald River – and I recalled the time I observed the safety practice of tagging and testing electrical equipment and the practical application of those red, green, blue and yellow tags.

> *"You were born with two ears, two eyes and one mouth. Use them in that order."*
> **My Dad**

CHAPTER 11

ARCI at Dugald River

ARCI is a decision and responsibility assignment matrix used in project management – and it is also the primary baseline that RUGBY Quality Review has been developed from.

☑ **Accountable**
☑ **Responsible**
☑ **Contributing**
☑ **Informed**

ARCI is used to identify the required participation from various roles to complete tasks or deliverables for a project or business process and it is especially useful in clarifying roles and responsibilities in cross-function / departmental projects and processes.

ARCI is an acronym derived from four key responsibilities most typically used are: *accountable*, *responsible*, *consulted* and *informed*.

RUGBY Quality Review recognises the four key responsibilities as: *accountable, responsible, **contributing** and informed.*

It is about now, I get to introduce to you another one of my top five people I thrived working with and learnt the most from in the five years I worked as a contractor on major projects.

I mentioned earlier that Dugald River was the first billion dollar construction project that I worked on. I had seen an ARCI matrix and understood the effectiveness of this very easily established and maintained *document* – but I had never seen it in play – I had never seen it demonstrated.

I say *demonstrated* because at Dugald River an ARCI matrix was not only a project management tool and capture. At Dugald River, I saw the ARCI project management discipline used by the Deputy Construction Manager as a communication tool. I'm not sure if he even realised that he baselined his decisions and conversations off this matrix. He's a smart guy – he probably did.

Using ARCI, he could readily identify if the personnel and external contractors working on the construction effort of the project were contributing appropriately on their responsibilities to deliver the project safely, on schedule, within scope and on budget.

Using ARCI, he could transparently communicate and address (where required), with any person or contractor working on the project, areas where they were not delivering on their identified *accountabilities, responsibilities* or *contributions* and he could always very effectively remind someone if their position on the deliverable was to merely be *informed*. Without question, everyone knew where he or she were identified and required to contribute from on this project.

Anthony Reynolds is one of my most favourite people to work with – I await the day he calls and says "Hey Kat – there's this project…"

I loved working with Tony because he was extraordinarily generous with his knowledge, experience and time – and he found himself a captive audience with me – because the knowledge and experience that he had to share, the way that he thought and the way that he worked was absolutely intriguing. He has a striking character, a commanding presence and an innate ability to keep everything and everyone on point.

Working with Tony was not all kittens and balloons though and it certainly did not start that way for me – I cried twice whilst I was working on that project. I cried once because Tony made me cry.

Awwww, now I have made him out to be the baddy in the story – so, I am going to share the reason why I cried so you can understand a RUGBY Mindset a little better – and so you can understand how effectively Tony used the ARCI project management matrix to communicate and get the best result for his employer, the project and the people who worked on the project with him.

The first time I cried on site, I think was within the first ten days of working with Tony.

I cried immediately following a 6.00 am daily pre-start meeting, a meeting where everyone shares the planned activities and deliveries of the day and important information related to safely delivering on the project.

I cried because not only was I out of my depth having never worked remote FIFO before and somewhat lonely on site, because I had not been out on site long enough to establish rapport or build relationships. I also at the time had no frame of reference to the discipline of ARCI and to Tony's innate ability to identify the true issue at hand and address it.

Wasted tears

A couple of days previous to the meeting that contributed to my wasted tears, I had returned to site from my rest and relaxation break (R&R) and was reviewing the fuel delivery schedule and reconciling them against the orders that had been placed.

It was during this administrative review that I identified that there was potential, that a fuel order had not been placed for delivery in the coming week, because I could not find any documentation to evidence or support that an order had been made.

I placed a call to the supplier, who advised that they had no record of an order being placed – *it turns out that an order had been placed so the information that I received was incorrect.*

I made some quick calculations against the current fuel load we had on site, against the highest daily consumption capture, to assess the potential that the site would run out of fuel, before the person who usually ordered the fuel returned to site from their R&R and placed an order if it was required.

Included in these calculations, I extrapolated the lead-time it would take for the fuel to be delivered after an order had been placed – Dugald River is in the middle-of-nowhere Australia, and the supply chain meant the fuel could take up to five days to arrive on site – and arrived at the conclusion that the site had potential to run low on fuel.

Armed with this information I raised it to Tony for his information and decision – which was, of course, to place a *conservative* order for fuel. Conservative, because if a fuel order had been placed (which it had) the fuel tanks on site would need to have capacity to hold any additional delivery load.

It was the first *obvious* example of a mitigated response I had seen demonstrated – I now know I had been sheltered in my previous corporate employment environments – working out in the harsh realities of remote north-western Queensland, I was introduced to a new perspective and a new approach to the considerations I needed to recognise and respond to in my job.

On the day the fuel delivery was expected to site, I provided the projected delivery in the daily prestart meeting, after which Tony asked:

"Can **someone** please tell me **why** an administrator identified this?"

So, I cried. I cried because I felt that my contribution in the project had been devalued by being identified as an 'administrator'. I cried because I was indignant – I remember thinking, "Oh you little shit! If I hadn't identified it – you could have had a problem." Moreover, I cried because my pride had taken a hit – and as with all things related to pride – the tears were of my own making. I was expecting praise and instead perceived criticism. Silly girl!

Reflection provided to me the reason why my tears were self-indulgent – because the question that Tony had asked was raised to address the true issue at hand.

Tony was asking – why? Why, out of all the people in the meeting that morning, who *should have known* and were *responsible to know*, if an order for fuel had been placed, why was the potential shortfall identified by an administrator, someone who was not responsible for the deliverable?

What Tony introduced to me that morning was his keen ability to identify contributors and hold them accountable or responsible by using ARCI. It was a good question and it got everyone on point. There was also a subtext in his question that morning, "I am situationally aware and I will hold to account."

I learnt one very good lesson from this event, one that I wish I had learned earlier in my career because it changed the way that I contribute and place value within my workplace now. I rarely leave myself vulnerable to seeking validation or praise. If I do, it is my own fault when I find myself bereft – and it speaks volumes to my own insecurities.

Tony **never** publicly praised any one person in the workplace, but he did in quiet moments where it was merited, recognise with you personally, if you were doing your job well and probably recommended you to his management peerage. Tony is an exceptional manager because he knows:

1. You are not employed to be praised for the work that you do – you are employed to deliver on your accountabilities and responsibilities and to meet the expectations of your employer.

2. If an employee is not meeting the accountabilities and responsibilities of their role or the expectations of their employer, they are not doing their job and it needs to be addressed for the success of the project or business.

3. By publicly praising any one person in the workplace, by showing preference towards another, you are introducing disharmony and an uneven playing field to the workplace or project and contributing towards that negative behaviour, unique to Australian culture, the 'Tall Poppy Syndrome'.

What Tony did do, if you were delivering on the accountabilities and responsibilities of your role, was support you. Unequivocally. If you were doing your job, the lad had your six.

One of the most admirable things about Tony, and this is something that I try to evidence in my own workplace behaviours, is that the decisions that he makes, the conversations that he has, *always* serve the best interest of his employer, the project that he is working on *and the people he works with*. When you are talking about billion dollar projects you want the *best people* working with you putting in their *best effort* – and Tony always brought out the best in people.

> *"You are not employed to be praised for the work that you do – you are employed to deliver on your accountabilities and responsibilities and to meet the expectations of your employer."*
>
> **Katrina Wilson**

CHAPTER 12

Red, Green, Blue and Yellow Tags at Dugald River

It was a very hot and dusty December day when I first observed one of the site electricians tagging and testing the electrical cabling around the site offices.

What I saw at the time was unremarkable. I saw the electrician test the electrical cable, remove the tag that was on it and replace it with another.

What did catch my attention was that the electrician had changed the colour of the tag from 'Yellow' to 'Red'.

It was a few months later that I saw the same electrician doing the same work again – moving about the site offices checking the electrical cabling and replacing the 'Red' tag to a 'Green' tag once his testing was complete – I recall my confusion as to why I was seeing him do a job that I had seen performed only a couple of months before – and I recall how curious I was to understand what I had observed.

So, at the next opportunity, which just happened to be at the Dugald River bar after work– I asked the electrician what he was doing that day and what the importance of the tags was. I laugh now as I recall the surprised look he threw my way, at what could only be considered such an obvious question with an obvious answer for anyone who is experienced in working on site.

Forgive my ignorance, and remember that I had not worked on site before, and before this day – I had always just gotten on with the job that I was paid to do – not giving too much thought to anyone else's job.

The electrician advised that he was 'tagging and testing the electrical cabling using the rugby system'. I was curious enough to mentally file the information away to google later – because I was not sure if the lad was having a lend of me or not, and because I did not want to appear more ignorant than I already felt.

I googled 'rugby system' after the next site daily project pre-start meeting (6.00 am morning meetings I do not miss!) and came up with… nothing. I concluded that if Google didn't know what it was – it was probably not worth knowing, and I started to think that the electrician had been pulling my leg after all.

But…. Google did suggest 'Did you mean RGBY?' By clicking on the suggested link, I read about a system that was used in the mining, construction and demolition industries in Australia that allowed for easy visual quarterly inspections for maintenance.

A few more clicks of my mouse, and I found buried within google, a site which further detailed that RGBY tagging was a system that had been developed with a safety focus and was required to be conducted on mine and construction sites in Australia and New Zealand for compliance with AS/NZS:3012 with the tagging captured to comply with AS/NZS:3760 standards.

The tagging code most commonly used in Australia is RGBY tagging, which can be captured as:

Red	Green	Blue	Yellow
DECEMBER	MARCH	JUNE	SEPTEMBER
JANUARY	APRIL	JULY	OCTOBER
FEBRUARY	MAY	AUGUST	NOVEMBER

A review of material from the internet does reflect different months assigned to the red, green, blue and yellow tag identifiers – so whilst the validity periods identified on these websites don't align – the tagging reflects what the practice promotes a valid period in time.

My attention was at once captured by how efficient the application of red, green, blue and yellow tags on electrical equipment was. It was amazing to me, how a job that had potential to be an extremely cumbersome and messy task, a job that had strong potential for something to be overlooked or missed was immediately transparent, agile and achievable with such a simple system.

I quickly realised that with a red, green, blue and yellow tag applied, anyone on site could pick up a piece of electrical cabling and identify if the equipment was safe and compliant for use, and that we could all sleep a little better at night knowing that identified risks had been mitigated in our high-risk job and work location.

As an example, the coloured tagging provides a means to identify if an electrical cable had been tagged and tested.

If there was no coloured tagging on the electrical cord or cabling, then the answer was no, the item had not been tested – and the equipment was not to be used.

If a coloured tag was applied, any person would be able to identify quickly if an electrical cord or cable had been tagged and tested in the last three months.

As an example, if the month was July and there was a red tag on the electrical cord – then anybody would know that the equipment had not been tested in the last three months and was not to be used.

One further advantage of this very simple system, and potentially its most significant advantage, was its very transparency.

In the case of tagging and testing on site, given the transience of the FIFO workforce, any electrician or suitably trained person could at any time continue to conduct seamless tagging and testing, without interruption, concern to safety, risk or cost to the project and anyone could identify if a piece of equipment was safe to use at any time.

Amazing! At the time, I had a passing thought in wondering if perhaps there was a way that this innovative safety approach could be developed further for a business to transparently identify and evidence risk, quality standards and continuity broadly across business.

CHAPTER 13

Battle Rhythm at Dugald River

For the first four months that I was working at Dugald River, I was the only administrator employed to administratively support the construction effort on site – which was appropriate because construction on the project was ramping up and was onboarding staff as the project schedule reflected.

What this meant was during this time my workload was increasing in proportion to the number of personnel and contractors as they onboarded to the project.

The number of hours that I was employed to work each day was ten, and the company, operations and construction management team of the project were very definite in maintaining that *no more* than ten hours were to be worked in any one day.

This was not a commercial decision. I and everyone else working on the project, was paid a day rate not an hourly rate – meaning that if we had worked more than ten hours – we would not have been paid for them.

It was not a commercial decision, because there would not be any further financial costs incurred to the project paid as overtime or time off in lieu.

The rigidity of working no more than ten hours a day was because the health and safety of the people working on the project was paramount. The construction of the project was as busy as any business reflects in peak periods – there was always more work that could be completed – but on this project the work associated to the construction effort needed to be completed in ten hours or less each day.

During that four months, as the construction effort ramped up, the site accommodated a compliment of external contractors to work on the civil earthworks and construction of the site village, the main access road, an airstrip and a bridge to cross the Dugald River.

To support these efforts, the company and project also employed construction superintendents, engineers, safety advisors, schedulers, contract managers, cost controllers, procurement managers, logistics managers and document controllers.

As the only site project construction administrator during that period, this captures as an ever-increasing workload that required me to deliver on the work I was responsible to deliver on that was planned for the day, and to be agile to respond to any additional work that may require attention from the environment external to the office – the construction effort.

Added to this busy workload was the consideration that I was employed to a 21/7 roster **which doesn't mean** that I *worked* for 21 days and had 7 days off as rest and relaxation (R&R).

There were other considerations that needed to be captured to accurately represent how many days I was productive on site:

- I had to travel for almost *one full day* to get to and from site. Travel for me, to and from site, meant taking a flight from Brisbane to Mount Isa and then driving to site, which captured as approximately eight hours in transit and no more than two hours in the office.

- On site, because the health and safety of people was paramount, no one was allowed to work more than 12 days *(I think it was 12 days)* without a fatigue day.

  The following captures visually for you an example of the days that I would have been productive on site on a 21/7 roster, compared against Head Office and introduce to you the structure that my battle rhythm would have aligned to.

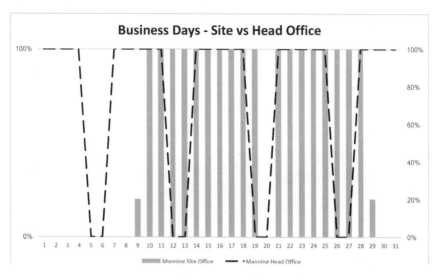

Business Days - Site vs Head Office

Location	Days Worked	Business Days	Productivity
Head Office	23	23	100%
Site Office	18	31	58%

Just for the fun of it – one last quick calculation – the number of days that my peer equivalent in head office worked, reflects as 23 productive days compared to my 18 productive site days. That's a difference of five business days – my counterpart in head office was present to attend to business approximately 20% longer than I was on site.

I developed a battle rhythm because as you can see from the roster above – averaging a 30-day month, I was only *on site to support* for approximately 60% of the time. The work continued to progress and accumulate for the balance 40%. In addition to that I had 20% less time to do the equivalent work that my counterpart in head office had.

Whilst I was not on site, the Site Operations Administrators were available to assist on urgent tasks that required attention, but they had their own work to do as well – so, I had to work smarter and with more efficiency and it was necessary to develop easy to follow processes if the project was to be supported appropriately – and function as business as usual – while I was off-site.

In doing this, I mitigated the potential of returning to a stressed workplace and a stressful workload.

Battle rhythm

A battle rhythm can be used to capture the significant milestones, contractual obligations, events and deliverables that regularly occur within your business or project. *A battle rhythm should not be used to capture the day-to-day deliverables of your role.*

Some examples on a project could be:

- Weekly meetings with contractors.

- Contractual response obligations. It may be a contractual obligation that minutes of a meeting must be formally issued from the owner to a contractor within 48 hours of a meeting.

- Reporting deadlines. A weekly report may be required to be submitted to head office by Monday of each week.

- Orders and deliveries. An order may need to be placed within a certain period if a delivery is to be received on time to site.

- Invoicing and financial reconciliation.

- Timesheets.

By establishing a battle rhythm, you can capture visually:

- Significant milestones, contractual obligations, events and deliverables.

- Peak activity periods.

- Deadlines that you can work back from to ensure you deliver on time.

- Your role priorities against your day-to-day deliverables.

- Deliverables that you will need to hand over to another person if you are unavailable.

> *"A battle rhythm can be used to capture the significant milestones, contractual obligations, events and deliverables that regularly occur within your business or project. **A battle rhythm should not be used to capture the day-to-day deliverables of your role.**"*
>
> **Katrina Wilson**

SECTION 3

Storming

CHAPTER 14

Challenging Bystander Apathy

One of the biggest challenges our society recognises today is bystander apathy – our human attempt at self-preservation – the conscious decision *to not be involved* in something that has the potential to disrupt our personal equilibrium, challenge our values or impact on our situation in life.

Bystander apathy exists in business too, but it is not called out for challenge as it is in society. What is interesting about bystander apathy in business is that the primary structure of a business actually promotes the behaviour.

I'm sure you are asking, how can a business's structure actively promote bystander apathy when society denounces the behaviour?

I call to your attention the primary visual tool that all businesses use to identify the structure of their organisation – what is commonly referred to as the 'Org Chart' – the graphical representation of an organisations or businesses structure.

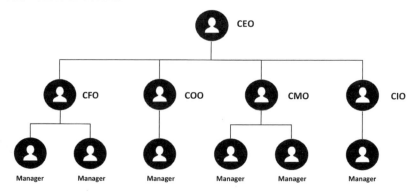

What information does an organisational chart seek to convey?

- You can identify the most senior person in an organisation and the subordinates that trail.

- The silos that exist within the business for it to function organisationally, which range from global classifications down to the departments or business functions of a business.

- Identification of your position within a business or organisation.

Business organisational charts are essential in business for it to function organisationally. What is often challenging for businesses about an organisational chart is the subtext that exists independent of the intent for which the structure has been developed, which is to support the growth and profit of a business.

The subtext that influences our business behaviours and how we contribute within it. The chain of command, our perception and recognition of the chain of command, how we respond to the chain of command and most specifically our human response and conscious decision *to not be involved* in something that has the potential to disrupt our personal equilibrium, challenge our values or impact on our situation in life.

The chain of command is important in business. It is important because the people who have been placed in positions we find ourselves subordinate to, have been placed in that position for a reason. Ideally, they have been placed in that position because they have been identified as the best person to lead, manage and achieve the results or outcomes that the business requires.

The chain of command is important because it provides to us the baseline of our influence and authority. A chain of command most certainly has its place in business to mitigate risk.

All of this makes sense. No one wants to make a decision that they are not qualified or supported to make. We know our place, we know the position from which we are required to contribute from and we know when we will be supported.

Bystander apathy occurs when all of these knowns become unknowns, when we are placed in a situation where we are required to make a decision or place ourselves into a position where we don't know if we will be supported or how much personal risk we will expose ourselves and the business to. When we find ourselves in this position, more often than not, we make a decision to *not be involved* and we tell ourselves that it is someone else's job, responsibility or problem.

What are the consequences if we choose to not be involved or participate as part of a solution to an event in the workplace? It's a broad sweep, but the cartoon below really captures more than words can say.

One area of business that challenges bystander apathy is around safe workplaces and safe work practices. The businesses that take safety seriously ensure that every employee, contractor or visitor knows and understands that unsafe work practices are never condoned and that every person is accountable and responsible for safety in the workplace.

The message is even stronger working in construction – every person working on-site knows and understands that they are accountable for their own safe work practices and responsible to stop any unsafe workplace practices.

Every employee on a construction site knows that they are *always* an active contributor in safety – because out on site the standard that you walk past, is the standard that you accept. What this means is that if you walk past a hazard or potential threat without isolating or removing it, if you ignore an unsafe practice without addressing it, you will be held responsible or accountable along with other contributors in the event.

You can't relay a stronger message than saying that everyone is responsible for safe work practices in the workplace.

Where the message weakens is in the behaviours we adopt when we attempt to align this crucial message with the organisational structure or the chain of command in business or on projects.

It weakens further when you introduce workplace politics, conflicting values and priorities and out on site, a stressed and delayed project schedule.

Before I started working at Moomba in South Australia, I was required to complete online inductions as directed by the site owner.

One of these inductions was a Safety Induction and the message that was very clearly provided by this company was an empowering and intimidating experience.

This company took safety so seriously, that they gave every employee, or contractor to site a card that we were required to carry with us as part of our identification.

This card stated "I, <name>, General Manager Engineering and Projects, authorise the holder of this card to stop any unsafe activity."

His message did not stop there. This leader and this company *recognised* that even though every employee or contractor on site:

- had completed the same online induction and had the same stop work card,

- knew they would be held accountable or responsible for safe work practices and environments on site,

- most certainly did not want to be the cause of a work injury or death,

they recognised a human's capacity for bystander apathy and self-preservation would always prevail. We have that capacity because we calculate the odds. What are the odds of something critical or catastrophic happening weighed against the political backlash I could unleash upon myself?

So, we enter that endless cycle of:

1. Doing nothing.

2. Feeling guilty about doing nothing.

3. Resolve to do something.

4. Recognise the potential negative impact to ourselves personally if we do get involved.

5. Do nothing.

6. Feel powerless.

feel powerless → do nothing → feel guilty → resolve to act → recognise potential (personal) negative impact → do nothing

This leader and this company recognised that sometimes people don't act or respond as quickly as they should because of political considerations, and our human need to protect ourselves and our livelihoods because *there is always going to be a bigger fish.*

So how did this leader and this company address this? By sending a very powerful message with a video and personal message as the final part of the online induction.

In this video the General Manager Engineering and Projects, once again identified how important safety was for the company and for the people who you work alongside and he closed the message off by stating firmly (I can't remember the exact words – but something along the lines of);

"If anyone makes a decision *in good faith* to stop work because of an unsafe activity they will be supported in their decision to stop the work, without concern to personal consequences."

I actually saw how effective this message was whilst I was on site, and I saw the very behaviours this message was voiced to address, when one of my colleagues (who was a superintendent and very experienced engineer) stopped work because he was concerned enough to identify it as an unsafe activity.

What happened next was the person who my colleague was subordinate to, thundered his indignance and fury at my colleague, and very loudly and publicly berated him for stopping the work, further challenging him by stating, "Who do you think you are? I stop the work around here – not you!"

Which I am sure you will agree is in direct contradiction of the intent and purpose of the site owner's safety message.

I love how my colleague chose to respond. With mustered dignity, my colleague turned around and respectfully advised, with an offhand waggle of his site safety 'stop work' card, "The General Manager Engineering and Projects of this site would support me in my decision." There's *always* a bigger fish!

Recalling this event on site was what lead me to recognising that being competent and confident in your workplace and the work that you deliver on, by recognising the position you have been identified to work from, provides any person the opportunity to pause and credibly identify, interrogate and respectfully respond to behaviours that contribute towards conflict in the workplace.

The first golden nugget that fell out of this research and this process.

Adopting a RUGBY Mindset focused towards identifying account-abilities, responsibilities and contributions removes the identity of a bully or a victim from the workplace by focusing on and addressing the behaviours that contribute to conflict.

In this particular event on site, essentially, my colleague was being bullied by his superior and his superior was evidencing his perceived dominance on site by belittling my colleague.

It occurred to me that the organisational silos that are necessary in business, are the reason why conflicts occur and innovation doesn't – because people will heavily fortify their perceived territory and defend it aggressively if challenged and they will respond to a documented chain of command.

What the General Manager Engineering and Projects of the site was effectively doing was stating that support would be given to any employee or contractor on site who were contributing / acting in good faith and responding to their accountabilities and responsibilities for the benefit of everyone.

He was supporting the employees and contractors on his site to identify and respectfully challenge and respond to bystander apathy.

> *"Adopting a RUGBY Mindset focused towards identifying accountabilities, responsibilities and contributions removes the identity of a bully or a victim from the workplace by focusing on and addressing the behaviours that contribute to conflict."*
>
> **Katrina Wilson**

CHAPTER 15

The Power of One

Probably one of the most influential experiences I have ever had, because of its similarities and parallels in business, and one of the most inspiring ways to demonstrate the success of challenging bystander apathy, is the measure of Dr Rolf Gomes and his vision for Heart of Australia.

In 'Heart Week' 2016 I attended a presentation and guest lecture hosted by the Women's Network of the University of Southern Queensland (USQ) which was held as a conversation with Dr Rolf Gomes. Dr Gomes is a medical practitioner specialising in cardiology and he is also the founder of Heart of Australia.

Not to put too fine a point on it, but Dr Rolf Gomes is an exceptional human being, as are the people who work beside him in his vision quest. He is a busy man. He is an important man. He is a man with a vision and a voice and he is a man who is influencing how healthcare is being delivered across Australia.

Generous. That would be a succinct word to capture the essence of the man who found time in his already busy schedule and commitments, to speak with the captivated audience at USQ to educate us on his vocation and introduce to us something that he is passionate about.

Rolf (we are on a first name basis now because I have met him once and this is my book) had many experiences to share with us, some funny, some tragic, and all of them collective in his vision of delivering specialist healthcare across Australia.

One of his shared stories truly resonated with me because I drew parallels from them and applied them to how many people approach or respond in their business or their job.

Of course, what follows will not be verbatim; what I write will be influenced by my own personal values and mindset, but I am pretty sure I've captured in essence what he said.

Rolf generously shared with us that which, as cardiologists he and his ilk are not too alarmed by, patients who present themselves (and I'm paraphrasing here), loudly declaring that they are short of breath, experiencing pain down the left side of their body and that it feels like an elephant is sitting on their chest.

Cardiologists and health practitioners, it would seem, are not too alarmed by this shared self-diagnosis, because the odds are reasonable to high that the patient is in fact experiencing a heart attack, and medical professionals are educated and trained to respond medically to this event.

Soberingly, Rolf shared with us that which made his stomach drop and caused him alarm, that being the response he sometimes received from a patient exhibiting, in his professional opinion, early indicators of cardiac distress.

His stomach would drop when, upon his recommendation of further testing or medical intervention, the occasional patient would advise that they were *too busy* or committed elsewhere to take time away from their business or livelihood to attend to his professional recommendation of medical testing, intervention or procedure.

I'm guessing that his stomach would drop because he sees daily that he can only help those who see themselves in a position to want to help themselves.

This resonated with me for the business parallel that I applied to his shared experience. What business parallel do you think I drew from this sobering story?

I drew that most people approach their career and business with the same priority that some of his patients approach their health.

That sometimes we are all so busy and focused on the day to day of business, with the distractions of business and lifestyle, that we fail to check in on our business health and only pay attention to something when the symptoms or events are too alarming not to address.

I also concluded that you can only help the people who want to help themselves.

It was this conversation, which ultimately contributed to a pause as I wrote this book, to cast a fresh eye over what I had written and developed with RUGBY, to create the opportunity for my readers to capture their own pause to critically assess and interrogate their business health.

In the following chapter, Rolf shares his story, his vision for healthcare in Australia and the shared vision he and his colleagues have for Heart of Australia. No one is better qualified in the telling, but here are a few things that I picked up during our 'conversation'.

Rolf's bio on the Heart of Australia website identifies him as a cardiologist, a father of three and principal of Medihearts – his established private cardiology practice in Brisbane, Australia.

His vision for Heart of Australia is committed through his Medihearts practice, to support his realisation in revolutionising the delivery of first-class specialist medical services to rural and remote communities.

It's a great bio capture for a website because of its integrity – but what it doesn't capture is the warmth and compassion of the man – and that you will only get to experience if you spend time in his company. That said, I will try to convey in my own words some of the things that are interesting about Rolf.

He emigrated from Calcutta with his family as a child.

He studied and practiced electrical engineering and then decided to study and practice medicine because he wanted to have more contact with people and to make a difference.

Professionally, he is an all-round electrician – he can take a look at any circuit board, electrical source or the electrical circuitry of a heart and know what needs to be done to mitigate and remedy any ailment. Sounds like a handy guy to have around, doesn't he?

He is also probably one of the bravest and smartest people you will ever be lucky enough to meet. *Brave.* Most definitely brave, because as he touched on as he was speaking, he sat across the table from his wife one day and said, "I'd like to make my vision for Heart of Australia a reality and to do that I need to take out a second mortgage on our home."

Smarts. He has smarts because he married an intelligent lady who shared his vision, knew it could become a reality and supported him, we know this because Heart of Australia exists and has achieved amazing success and saved many lives in the years since its inception.

He has smarts because he knew that he could not achieve what he wanted to achieve without sacrifice, brave conversations, contribution and beneficiation of others and sponsorship.

So, what is Heart of Australia now that that the vision is a reality? It's a mindset focused on priorities. It is also a purpose-built, self-sufficient and custom designed 25 metre long trailer clinic on wheels, driven by passion and a Kenworth K200 prime mover.

Right now, Heart of Australia embraces an innovative approach to medicine which is transforming how healthcare is delivered to, and across rural south-east and central Queensland. Heart of Australia deploys a specialist team of cardiologists to go to the patients who have limited access to specialist care and who also may not fully understand their own risks.

Rolf's vision for the future is to provide these specialist services and others across all remote locations of Australia.

I encourage you all to visit their website www.heartofaustralia.com. The website provides to you visually what Heart of Australia is right now and it titillates you in envisioning what Heart of Australia will be in the future.

It is important to remember as you are perusing the site, that everything captured in that single .com url thread started with compassion, came to life and is nurtured by a vision and became a reality through passion, sacrifice, hard work, philanthropy and sponsorship. And, it started with one person who challenged inequity, promoted an idea and provided a solution to ensure their vision for others became a reality.

> *"Your success is dependent upon how much accountability and responsibility you place upon yourself equally balanced with how much you contribute."*
>
> **Katrina Wilson**

CHAPTER 16

Highway to Health

Heart of Australia – Making a Difference

There are many things we do in life but what are the things we do that really matter in the end. What are the things, which we will reflect on as our greatest achievements – success in business, a happy family life, children we are proud of?

In my role as a cardiologist I have had the privilege of being at the bedside of many patients, who when faced with the reality that life's day is turning into night have shared with me what has for them ultimately mattered in the end. There are two recurring themes. Family and achievement. Whilst the joys of a close and happy family are understandable, what is revealing is the lasting pride and comfort that achievement, quite distinct from wealth, imparts upon the individual. In fact, I have come to the conclusion that what matters in the end can be measured not by what we have acquired but by what we have accomplished.

I have always allowed myself time for introspection as I believe it is essential for clear thinking. Consider this. Have you ever been faced with a hard decision? If so, why was it hard? Was the decision itself hard or the consequences of making the right decision hard? In our own quiet moment, our conscience eventually reveals the answer. The courage to pursue the right decision is then what defines our character. Sometimes a task seems impossible but what is it that makes it impossible? The lack of a solution or the courage and stamina to pursue a solution? Perhaps I am fortunate to have begun my professional life as an Engineer adhering to the engineering mantra that 'Engineers make it happen'. Certainly, this approach has allowed me on many occasions to whittle down a seemingly impossible problem to manageable tasks but there is something else, and that something else is the courage to take the first step. To accept that a perfect solution does not pre-exist but is revealed as we persevere.

I believe The Heart of Australia program embodies our finest attributes. Compassion, creativity and our capacity for hard work. They say man's mind once stretched never goes back to its original dimensions and as a junior doctor working in rural and remote parts of Australia I was often confronted by the lack of specialist services, many of which, city people take for granted. For myself, addressing this inequity began with accepting the reality that as a practicing specialist I was inherently required to be a part of the solution – leadership by example. My engineering past soon resurfaced and I began to wonder if these services could be encapsulated into a mobile entity and delivered to rural communities on a large scale. What followed was six years of sweat and hard labour eventually culminating in the launch of the Heart of Australia mobile cardiac clinic on the 3rd of October 2014.

At present the Heart of Australia clinic-on-wheels travels 8,000 kilometres a month delivering life-saving cardiac and respiratory services to access-disadvantaged patients in twelve rural communities across the state of Queensland. Since the launch of the program eighteen months ago over 2,000 patients have been treated and at least eighty lives have been saved. Referrals to the program are growing rapidly and the need to expand has already arrived. What previously seemed impossible is now possible and a testament to the truism that everything mankind has ever created began with a thought. For myself and the Heart of Australia program it is hard to know exactly what that first thought might have been but I do recall that first step….one quiet night after my three young children, Jacqueline, Lenny and Patrick had gone to bed switching on the light and sketching the floor-plan of a truck.

I invite you to join us on the highway to health at:

www.heartofaustralia.com

– Dr Rolf Gomes, Heart of Australia

> *"Everything mankind has ever created began with a thought."*
>
> **Dr Rolf Gomes**

CHAPTER 17

Quality
– The Heart of Your Business

This chapter captures the business parallel I assigned against Dr Gomes's share, where an occasional patient would delay their response to his professional recommendation of further testing or medical intervention that could improve their current health or contribute to a longer life.

Why is it that Rolf would, upon occasion, have his specialist medical opinion overlooked if it is a human's basic instinct to survive? We make decisions every day to maintain this objective – our instinct to survive. Where I think we are challenged is when we fail to assess and refocus our priorities – not because we are too lazy to do so – but because we believe we will have more time in the future.

It's the same in business – we often put something off for another day, we overlook an emerging priority – because we don't find the time to assess and refocus our shifting business exposure – unless something untoward occurs, then that's all we have time for.

When something untoward occurs in business, we are required to respond to something that we may have had an inkling about occurring, but considered the immediate risk of the event occurring as low or even acceptable.

When something untoward occurs in life and in business, we rarely respond with "Wow! Didn't see that one coming", we almost always invariably experience regret and personally chastise ourselves for overlooking or ignoring something that we should have seen coming.

We find ourselves in this position, not because we don't have time but because we don't place value. *We don't have to find time to attend to the things that we value.*

It's a chicken or the egg conundrum. It's not important which came first, *it's important that we recognise that the egg may not exist without the chicken and the chicken may not exist without the egg.*

Likewise, the symbiotic relationship between quality management practices and business. It's not important which comes first, it's important that we recognise that a business **would not** exist without quality management practices and quality management practices **exists** independent of any one business.

Quality should be the heart of your business, because quality is and always will be *bigger than any one person or business.* **Quality is a global discipline.** Resistance to quality and quality management systems is futile – what you resist persists and what you embrace dissolves.

As what you resist persists, attempting to push certain experiences away only serves to draw more of the same to yourself. Through focusing on what we don't want, we attract more of it.

Recognising that quality is a global discipline will aid you as your business grows – but it probably won't inspire the people who you either work alongside or who you employ. Why? Because in most cases, the big picture of quality, its costs and its risks mean very little if anything to them personally.

So how can you get some heart into how quality is nurtured in your business by your employees? How can you help people to find the time to pay some attention to the quality needs of your business?

- Remember that no one ever needs to find time for something they consider a priority.

- Recognise that people will not purposefully apply themselves in a project or in the workplace if they don't have a baseline to establish themselves from.

If you make quality and quality management practices the baseline, the recognised minimum standard that everyone is to work towards achieving, you will have something to measure success or failure against.

Quality is the heart of your business because, if there is no heart in your workplace there is no function or purpose and nothing to aspire to or contribute towards.

Without quality, a person has no heart or pride for the work they are doing – because we all like to work towards being the best we can possibly be and we all like the recognition of success.

> *"If you make quality and quality management practices the baseline, the recognised minimum standard that everyone is to work towards achieving, you will have something to measure success or failure against."*
>
> **Katrina Wilson**

CHAPTER 18

Why Quality is so Important for Your Business

We've touched on quality being the heart of your business, now it is important to touch on why quality is so important for your business.

Quality is important for business because it has a cost. If a consumer is not happy with the quality of a product or service that your business provides – they will take their custom elsewhere – which affects a business's cash flow and marketable brand.

Quality however is so much bigger than a consumer service industry focus because a business or nations economic welfare and survival depends upon the quality of the goods and services they produce.

Additionally, quality or the evidenced lack of quality review, process and procedure contributes towards another industry, which is completely independent of quality and quality management practices. The industry of civil litigation, insurances, legal representation, lawsuits, establishing legal precedence and the rigmarole of 'he said', 'she said', 'prove it'!

John Knapton, who wrote the foreword for this book, is recognised as an international legal expert because of his experience in forensically investigating failure and identifying the contributing factors that indicate towards its point of origin.

His success and recognition is because of his ability to forensically review and identify why something fails, in being able to critically communicate and credibly argue or defend in a court of law, why a failure occurred.

He forensically investigates, to identify the contributing factors of why a failure occurred and his expert opinion is sought to determine if a business can be held accountable for the failure.

To do this he:

- Recognises the authority of what is internationally recognised and legally defined as best practice, the *minimum standard* that **must be met** for the design, work or product to be considered compliant or fit for purpose. An international governing standard.

  This is particularly important because if a standard doesn't exist, then there is nothing to baseline or measure from, therefore nothing to argue for or against and nothing to defend.

- Reviews the integrity of a business demonstrating the way they conduct their business against the way *they say they conduct their business.* Evidencing from the process and procedures, the checks and balances a business has in place, which are usually interrogated against and recognised through ISO certifications.

  This is particularly important because if a business doesn't conduct itself against the baseline it has been accredited to contribute from then, there is nothing to support and only ever something to defend.

It is these two considerations in a lawsuit, which will ultimately decide on whether a business is solely accountable for a failure, or not.

Primarily, it is recognising and addressing these two considerations that will allow a business to mitigate one of its greatest risks – its ability to deliver on something it is certified to deliver on.

A business can ensure best practice, it can deliver from a minimum identified standard through its discipline, focus and demonstrated use of the quality management practices it has been certified for.

To put it bluntly, but with the greatest respect for John and his peers, John's profession and area of expertise exists in the international legal landscape because in business, employers and employees address their present business, without giving too much thought to future implications, or any consideration at all to the past – unless something bad happens.

Our business future is exciting because it presents potential of where we can be and we can work towards achieving or attaining something. The past is often overlooked in business because we relegate the experience to an event, something that we cannot change and something that we move forward from.

John once provided this little gem of an observation when we shared a conversation.

Our business future is a continuum of time and space that we have no concept or clue of.

So, if our past is something that we move forward from and our future is something that we move towards – what exactly is our present? We don't often ask ourselves exactly what that is or even challenge what that should look like – because we are participating in something in that moment without consideration to our past or our future.

Take a minute to cast your mind back to the evolution of business in the last 20 years. If you identify as an upcoming generation of business leaders, take some time to interrogate the evolution of business in the last 20 years and be afraid, be very afraid – it will fortify you in the future.

In closing I offer the view that our business past is something that we fail to accurately capture to review, stabilise or develop from, because of the transient and fluctuating nature of how we genuinely recognise and deploy our workforce.

This is where a RUGBY Mindset lends some opportunity for pause in business to conduct a health check, to ensure that the heart of its business, its quality supported by its quality management practices, is as healthy as it needs to be, to not only survive but thrive.

RUGBY Quality Review provides a visual cue that creates an opportunity for a person to pause to:

- Credibly review if all the information is currently correct.

- Capture change and other actions to mitigate potential for error to occur in the future.

To close out this chapter it is important to recognise that mistakes are going to be made and errors are going to occur. What is important is to focus your business approach towards making the fewest mistakes.

Like the game of rugby, the success and growth of your business hinges on:

- How you capture and then respond to these mistakes and errors to level your business playing field, gain a competitive edge and profit.

- If the competition is evenly balanced it is the business that makes the fewest errors that gains the competitive edge.

- If the competition is unbalanced, if a smaller business is competing against a bigger business, if they can be strategic in their capture and respond to change, a small business can narrow the gap by working towards making fewer mistakes and mitigating potential for future errors to occur.

What is the current state of health of your business? The business that you own or the business that you are employed in? When was the last time that you undertook an unbiased and forensic review of its health and most importantly identified the position from which you contribute within it?

Is it time to take some time to check in and address that which our busy work days and life have contributed to us overlooking?

Is it time for us to check in on our business health, the heart of our business, and focus on identifying symptoms or events which are too alarming not to address?

Is it time for us to have a look back on all the lessons learned to profit from some of the money and time we have already spent and invested in developing ourselves and business?

> *"Our business future is a continuum of time and space that we have no concept or clue of."*
>
> **John Knapton**

CHAPTER 19

Battle Rhythm

What I know about a battle rhythm I either have learnt from my mentor Bill Thomson through his advice, through my own observations of people in the workplace, or have identified myself from reading the contemporary books written on Sun Tzu's military principles.

To my way of thinking a battle rhythm is about:

- Being situationally aware.

- Recognising your terrain.

- Being agile to respond.

- Seeing opportunities where others see adversity.

This business style and discipline promotes situational awareness, and I share with you an experience that occurred whilst I was working with Bill, around the time the global financial crisis was starting to affect businesses in Australia.

This example will provide to you a frame of reference as to how effective a battle rhythm is in the workplace to be agile in your response.

The global financial crisis heralded a tough time for business globally; it was a tough time *for people* everywhere. News reports led with many country's currencies in freefall, plummeting stock prices and interviews with people who were living in their cars – because their homes had been repossessed. Family units broke down. Suicides occurred. Crime increased. Depressing.

If that isn't enough of a warning of what was heading our way in Australia, I don't know what was. Australia itself was somewhat insulated because at the time we were in the middle of what many termed the 'mining boom', but that boom, would as we all know eventually end in a bust, and the natural resource commodity prices would eventually drop – which we now know has occurred.

The global financial crises did eventually hit our shores and like a cyclone it hit hard and fast. The company I was working for at the time, made up to 20% of their workforce redundant before 11 am. People who had gotten out of bed that morning and presented themselves to work found themselves unemployed by lunchtime.

As professionally and efficiently as the management of this company conducted the off-boarding and release of personnel that morning, it could not stop the tide of stress, tears, guilt and anxiety.

Stress and tears because we are human and it is a human response to recognise that the people who were released unceremoniously, were our friends, peers and colleagues – people we had a relationship with – and their world and sense of self-worth had just been turned upside down.

Guilt because we still had a job and did not immediately face an uncertain future.

Anxiety because the work that had once been completed by the many staff who were no longer there, now needed to be completed by the staff who remained.

At the time, I too was experiencing the gamut of human emotion, so although I might have been subconsciously processing everything that was going on around me I was in survival mode and doing the things that needed to be done to survive.

Time, of course, always provides to us an opportunity for reflection and although I have never sat down and actually shared a conversation with Bill on this event in our work history, I now recognise that Bill had actually started developing and implementing a battle rhythm six to nine months *before* the event.

Some of the decisions that Bill made in this time I can now see with absolute clarity. Bill introduced me to the concept of being *situationally aware*. Until I met him I had never even heard the turn of phrase and hindsight affords me recognition.

Because of his professional background and training, Bill has the ability to recognise the significance of something that everyone perceives, and he responds and makes decisions to mitigate the casualty and attrition rate.

When the global financial crisis loomed and beckoned at our business shores Bill registered its potential, planned for and chose his response.

Bill saw what everyone else saw. He had the same information that everyone else had – that the world was experiencing a global financial crisis and that Australian businesses would not be immune from the impacts, mining boom or not. He recognised what was coming, and he started making decisions to minimise its impact. He made decisions that navigated the operations business unit he was responsible for towards a less hostile or rugged terrain – not only providing some shelter or succour from the eventual fallout for the people he managed, he also strategised to ensure that the business could adjust and buoyantly weather.

Bill is a technology leader with an Australian Army engineering and geospatial background, who has an educated, trained and innate ability to recognise his terrain – incidentally, this is one of Sun Tzu's principles.

Whilst others in the business were employing more staff and expanding, Bill was not renewing contractor positions and not replacing staff as they resigned, Bill was narrowing the focus of his team and expanding on our ability to work more efficiently.

Contractors as we know are expensive. Contractors are usually engaged to support a critical need in a business; because they are specialists whose skills are only required either to meet a specific deliverable or purpose or to provide support during peak business periods – and Bill recognised this.

By not replacing the staff who left, he was also instilling with purpose in his team our ability to be agile in choosing our response and to be consistent and efficient in our business as usual approach.

His leadership **expected** that although the team had contracted, the business unit would continue to perform and deliver as efficiently, if not more efficiently, than it had prior to the staff members' departure. It brings to mind the old adage that no one is irreplaceable. It resonates with me to this day – understanding this is why I enjoyed my tenuous experiences as a contractor on major projects, where I found myself employed and summarily unemployed when a project halted, and why my personal business philosophy is to leave an employer in a better condition than which I found them in.

So, whilst I don't want to rewrite a history I don't have any knowledge of, I would place safe money on betting that whilst the other managers in the business were, at that time, sitting down with a list of employees and making decisions on who they were going to need to reluctantly identify for redundancy, Bill was advocating to maintain the employees that he was responsible for, and supporting them by evidencing his strategic contraction of the business unit over the previous months. I'll have to ask him one day, over a shared bottle of red.

One of the most significant things I have learnt from Bill is to see opportunities where others see adversity.

Where some may see:

- More work because a contributing peer was not replaced, others would see an opportunity to expand on their knowledge and skillset.

- Less time to deliver on the work that they were responsible for, others would see an opportunity to introduce and implement new work strategies to become more efficient.

- Their hourly pay rate drop as their working hours increased, others might see the opportunity to *increase* their hourly pay rate by getting their work completed efficiently.

My personal opinion is that the people who see opportunity where a business can best profit, are the outliers in business, if you can harness their point of difference, because when times are tough you need to work with more smarts and focus, not just cut overhead and costs.

Outliers are the people who don't follow the S-Curve, the people who don't follow the flock, and the people who are often identified as an anomaly, difficult, overlooked and dismissed out of hand.

Having worked with Bill, I now look to identify the people who are outliers in business. To identify what is different about that person, to identify how the way they work and think, makes them different from everyone else. To benefit personally by identifying what makes them successful and then develop some of their skills, knowledge or perspective into my own skillset.

One final question or thought as I close off this chapter. Where did all the money that was lost during the global financial crisis go? Even if you were to write off 80% of these catastrophic losses against futures, stock prices, global currencies and an inflated housing market, the remaining 20% is still a considerable amount to account for.

I can't help but think that somewhere out there in the world exists a small number of people and businesses who recognised that a global financial crisis loomed and were smart and agile enough to be pre-emptive. I don't know – I don't recall any one business or person in that period proudly declaring that they mitigated their losses or made a motza off the global financial crisis – but I think that some people did.

I hope from this chapter you are now considering shaping your mindset towards developing in yourself personally, and within your business the ability to:

- Be situationally aware.

- Recognise your terrain.

- Be agile in your response.

- See opportunities where others see adversity.

- Identify the outliers in your business to profit.

> *"Identify the outliers in your business to profit and to capture a competitive edge."*
>
> **Katrina Wilson**

CHAPTER 20

Can't see the Forrester
for the Trees

Dear readers, I introduce to you one of the people I have enjoyed working with the most, one of the people who I have learnt the most from and the person who, only *after* I no longer had the honour of calling colleague, I reflected on not only her valuable skillset but her remarkable work–life perspective. I enjoyed working with her so much that, if I could have when I left our shared employment environment, I would have put her in my pocket and taken her with me.

I started developing my own concept of a personal battle rhythm by working with Bill but I learnt how to focus my attention and therefore my time and work-life balance from working with a young lady by the name of Donna Forrester.

She hails from 'Generation Y' which immediately follows mine, 'Generation X', and for a very short period of time, until I was mature enough to recognise and appreciate our differences, it was both fascinating and frustrating to work with Donna.

My personal challenge when first working with Donna was because her perspective and approach in business was directly influenced by the values aligned with and assigned by the generation from which she was nurtured, and they were in direct contradiction to the values aligned and assigned to mine.

I truly started to benefit from my professional association and then my friendship with Donna when I realised that our contributions within the workplace were a direct result from **nurture and not nature** and that by combining the values, focus and skills that we both maintained, we captured the symbiotic cadence of mentoring that breached a generation gap.

Donna is an amazing procurement administrator. She is one of the people who inadvertently influenced and challenged me, because she understood *exactly* what the often-promoted business concept of a work–life balance is and worked exceptionally within that frame.

My model of a personal battle rhythm is a direct result of observing what she executes so successfully in the workplace.

Some of the things I love about Donna:

- Nothing seems to faze her – and this is because Donna has a highly developed sense of self. She knows what she has influence over and doesn't concern herself with the things that she has no influence over. This is what makes her so unique, because she focuses her attention on the things that she can influence and will be held accountable for.

- She turned up for work each day and delivered on the work that she was responsible for – nothing was ever in delay because of anything that she was working on. If you ever had a question as to the status of something, she always had an update for you.

- Because she completed her work so efficiently and successfully she always had time to help you – *if you asked her for help*. You had to ask for help – and this is a positive capture – because she knew the value of her own time.

- She managed her current and forecast workload and knew if she had the skills and capacity to assist. And, she was smart enough to not establish a precedent that she would assist if you were being lazy in addressing the work that you were responsible and paid to deliver.

One of the biggest things I learnt from working with Donna was not to contribute towards a false economy of who does what in the office. What I mean by this is just because someone doesn't look busy – *doesn't* mean that they are *not busy* delivering on their job. Conversely, just because someone *does* look busy it doesn't mean that they *are* busy delivering on their job.

I still recall the day, one of our peers in the office complained loudly that they already had too much work, when they were asked to work on something that they were responsible and paid to do. Their response at the time was 'get Donna to do it – she's not busy'.

I was disappointed and annoyed to hear that response at the time, and this kind of response still irks me to this day, because I have heard the same phrase used in other workplaces since, and the subtext is still the same.

Why was I disappointed and annoyed and what was the subtext?

I was disappointed and annoyed because by deflecting, that person was not only objecting to delivering on a job that they were responsible for, and paid for by the business to deliver on, they were at the same time casting doubt as to Donna's **value and contribution** in the workplace.

Coincidentally, right before I submitted this manuscript to the publishers, I had the opportunity to enjoy a meal and the company of Donna and her husband, and she shared with me then what I am sure you are expecting to read now, that she continues to experience the same behaviours and attitudes in the workplace.

She shared with me a conversation that she had with one of her previous managers, who called a meeting with her to respond to a complaint that one of her peers had made – in that *every time* they looked at her computer monitor she was 'surfing the net'. Every time?

Her manager it seemed, and as they advised her at the time, was struggling to address the issue or concern, because they recognised that Donna always had her work completed and to the high standard that she always works to. The outcome of the conversation? Donna was asked to not spend *so much time* on the internet.

This is my opinion and not Donna's – but here's the funny, actually I find it hilarious – Donna's role at the time was in procurement, and knowing Donna she would have been spending most of that time 'surfing the net' in research.

It begs the question. As a procurement officer, would it not make sense in *considering* that it was in her (and her employer's) best interest to be aware of what was available and emerging in our global market to compare and produce a gap analysis?

It begs a further question. Was the issue her manager was struggling to address, the real issue? Probably not – but it was presented as an *obvious issue to address* from the disgruntled employee who made the complaint.

I wouldn't know, I wasn't there, but I would suggest that the real issue should have been in recognising the value that Donna contributed in the workplace, *as an outlier in the business*, with that feedback provided back to the disgruntled employee who complained, and not the management remonstration Donna found herself on the other end of.

A win–win would have been assured had the manager chosen that response and not the lose–lose that resulted.

I hope from this chapter you are now considering shaping your mindset towards developing in yourself personally, and within your business the ability to:

- Focus your attention on the things that you can influence and will be held accountable for.

- Interrogate the prejudice that can exist in a workplace – just because someone *doesn't* look busy does not mean that they're not busy delivering on their responsibilities.

- Don't contribute towards a false economy of deliverable distribution in the workplace. Lazy or inefficient people in the workplace should be identified for additional training – not propped up by others.

- Recognise the real issues and concerns and choose your response.

- Identify and profit from the outliers in your business.

> *"Don't contribute towards false economy of deliverable distribution in the workplace. Lazy or inefficient people in the workplace should be identified for additional training – not propped up by others."*
>
> **Katrina Wilson**

CHAPTER 21

Situational Awareness

Situational awareness contributes to underlining many of Sun Tzu's philosophies and it is something that I learned from working with Bill Thomson and from my experiences as a contractor.

I have observed that the best employees on a project and within a business are the employees who are competent and comfortable within their terrain, and not only comfortable within the terrain.

With the rapid expansion and contraction of business nowadays, a business can profit most if they employ people who are competent within their work environment and not just comfortable within it.

There are no guarantees in business, or life for that matter, but many employees attribute a permanent full-time continuing position within a company, as some form of guarantee. These employees quickly become complacent and leave themselves resistant and vulnerable to change. *I hate to burst your bubble, but the only things that can be guaranteed in life are death and taxes.*

When a business needs to contract to survive, a business owner or leader will cut overheads and then make employees redundant. Although not pleasant, it is a fact that we all know exists, because we have either observed or experienced redundancy during the global financial crisis period and in business since, as our business world adjusts and responds to conflict, changing needs and technology.

An employee, whose mindset is weighted towards being competent and comfortable within their work environment, knows and plans to be agile to respond in business, and adjusts to **not be** dependent on that employer or environment. *A competent employee keeps their eyes and ears open to be situationally aware of what is going on around them.*

An employee, who identifies their workplace as comfortable find themselves complacent towards the business that employs them. They are the people who turn up to work each day and do their job. They are the people who turn up to work each day and don't do their job. They are the people who 'face-time' in the workplace.

Employees who are comfortable in their environment don't want to experience change. They want everything to stay the way it always has been to continue their comfortable existence and routine. Employees who are comfortable in their work environment, who don't want anything to change, are often the people who demonstrate the most resistant and negative behaviours when the potential for change is raised, and when change occurs; and they are the employees who will contribute toward the churn that stops innovation.

The potential for change can be raised just by asking the most uncomplicated questions. Why do we do this that way? Is this the best way to do this? Whose job is it to deliver or work on this?

I often ask these questions at work, not because I want to make more work for someone, challenge them in some way or question their value. I ask these questions, because they are **very** good questions to ask in business. I ask these questions, because I don't know the answer, and I am asking these questions of someone who I think might know the answer.

"Why do we do it this way?" The best response anyone could receive to this question would be: because of safe work practices; compliant quality practices; governing regulations; business policy or because it has been reviewed and identified as best practice for the business.

I have never received any of these responses to my question though. Why? Probably because the person I asked is not aware of any of these business considerations. That being the case, I am asking the right questions from the wrong person.

Generally, the response that I receive is something along the lines of "It's the way we've always done it." When I hear this response, I know immediately that I am having a conversation with a *comfortable employee*, someone who is comfortable in their workplace and doesn't want anything to change.

I have experienced some hard lessons in the subtle dance of workplace culture, silos and politics before I came to identify this employee type – the *comfortable employee*. When I ask "Why do we do it this way?" to a *comfortable employee*, I rightly or wrongly (I think wrongly) am immediately identified as difficult and they see the question as a challenge to them personally.

When I ask this question of people who are situationally aware, familiar and confident in who they are, competent in the work that they do and comfortable in their environment, the response I receive to my question is different – I have identified these people as a *competent employee*. A competent employee will develop the question towards a conversation, and see it as an opportunity to ask themselves the same question "Why **do** we do it this way?"

By asking this question and turning it towards a conversation it always leads to a second question.

"Is this the best way to do it?" I have learnt that there is little benefit in leaving myself vulnerable to asking this second question with a *comfortable employee* because it only cements in their mind, that their first character assignment they have made to me, as a result of my first question, is that I am most definitely difficult and I am indeed challenging them.

My amygdala response (the part of our brain that kick's into overdrive as soon as our survival instinct is roused, where our response is either fight or flight) in this situation is heavily weighted towards flight – to preserve my professional hide and my personal brand and integrity – because it is my experience that posing this somewhat innocuous question to a comfortable employee *results in absolute shut down* – and there is no potential for business improvement or innovation in absolute shutdown – once again I am asking the right question from the wrong person.

Short this side of hell freezing over, there is nothing I could do or ask that would ameliorate this relationship, or persuade this person towards the generous consideration of wanting to work with me in the future – because the answer is **not interested**.

I am reluctant to waste my time in asking any more questions of a *comfortable employee*. Nevertheless, if the question has merit and potential to improve or innovate, I might be brave enough to dip my toe into that newly introduced political quagmire, at the risk of having to fortify and defend my personal brand and integrity.

There is a quantifiable loss in choosing flight though, an opportunity that is not passed over by a *competent employee*. It is the lost opportunity to credibly review and assess, if the current way the job is being delivered, aligns to: safe work practices, compliant quality practices, governing regulations; business policy; as best practice **and** *has potential for the business to capture new opportunities, benefit, profit or identify risk broadly across the business*.

By asking the question *"Is this the best way to do it?"* you are creating an opportunity to review, innovate and influence positive change, for the business to reinforce, reinvigorate, improve, further profit and remain agile.

This is why most businesses struggle with change – because the culture that their business nurtures is one of comfort and not competence.

"Whose job is it to deliver on this?" Probably one of the most conflicting questions I ask and one I have learnt that you **never** ask a *comfortable* *employee.* If you ask this question of a *comfortable employee* – they will respond to a completely different question to the one that was actually asked, which was "Whose job is it to deliver on this?" – because they unequivocally attribute the question to an attack, the person asking the question is challenging them personally.

This question is probably one of the most important questions to ask, because more often than not no one has actually been identified to be accountable or responsible for the job.

A comfortable employee doesn't care whose job it is – what is important to them is that they don't think it is their job (even if it is).

*A competent employee knows that if someone has been identified as accountable or responsible for the job, then the question would **not** exist – because the job would be getting done.*

The fact that the question does exist identifies a potential point of failure in a business, project or process and it *should* be addressed – but it often is not because of the conflict it raises in the workplace amongst *comfortable employees.*

When the number of comfortable employees far exceeds the number of competent employees in a workplace – you can be **assured** that your business will operate and be managed the way that it always has, with little or no opportunity of change, growth or a competitive edge.

So what are the similarities and differences between a *comfortable employee* and a *competent employee*?

A *comfortable employee* **is not** confident in their workplace because they are not situationally aware and don't recognise that their contribution towards ensuring the success and profit of their employer is directly attributed to a growth mindset.

A *competent employee* **is** confident in their workplace because they are situationally aware and they know that their contribution towards ensuring the success and profit of their employer is directly attributed to their growth mindset.

In closing, remember that any successful businessperson or entrepreneur always leads and succeeds by being brave enough to take him or herself out of their comfort zone and challenge their environment to capture opportunities and identify risk.

> *"A successful businessperson or entrepreneur always leads and succeeds by being brave enough to take him or herself out of their comfort zone and challenge their environment to capture opportunities and identify risk."*
>
> **Katrina Wilson**

CHAPTER 22

The Science of
RUGBY Quality Review

RUGBY Quality Review has as part of its foundation principles the science and psychology of two studies conducted by psychologists in the early twentieth century.

The first study identified is the Zeigarnik Effect (circa 1927) which identifies our human tendencies to no longer pay attention to something that we consider completed and the second study identified is 'Pavlov's Theory' or 'Pavlov's Dog's (circa 1902) which identifies as classical conditioning or learned behaviours.

These two studies and perspectives have shaped RUGBY Quality Review to capture human behaviours that, when recognised, will support the business process and the technology that is RUGBY Quality Review.

RUGBY Quality Review premises from the baseline of recognising that the introduction and implementation of a business process or technology, in isolation to considering the people who will be using it, will never lead to successful endorsement, adoption, integration or promotion in a workplace – because we humans have an element to us that technology cannot replicate – and that is a will.

If something is too hard or cumbersome, if we humans don't know where to start on something – we will exert our will and determination – simply by not using something, not using something for the purpose or intent it has been established for or by not contributing.

Therefore, we humans regress to thinking that it is not our job but someone else's – because if we don't want to do it – we deflect attention elsewhere and make it someone else's problem, which in the world of major projects reflects 'churn' and in the business world reflects 'conflict' – both have a financial burden applied.

These two studies are a fascinating read – if you have the time and inclination – transport yourself down the Google rabbit hole, and have a look at some of the interesting perspectives published on these theories. Following, I have captured my understanding of what these studies are about.

The Zeigarnik Effect

The Zeigarnik Effect is a result of the research and observations conducted by Lithuanian psychologist Bluma Zeigarnik in the effect of interruption on memory processing.

It was while studying at the University of Berlin that her professor noted how wait staff in a café seemed to remember uncomplete (or current) transactions more efficiently than those transactions that had been concluded or completed – which suggests that if a person considers a task or job complete it could lead to it being forgotten.

What this means is that whilst the wait staff still had customers to transact with, to take their orders, to clear their table and to finally collect payment from, the wait staff recalled clearly the duties that they were required to perform and execute.

Once the wait staff considered their transaction with a customer complete, they forgot about it, because their focus was on their next customer's needs.

It is about finished business and unfinished business, and how we humans compartmentalise to move forward.

As an example, the Zeigarnik Effect is used to great effect by media. It's the cliff-hanger at the end of serial, the one that has you on tenterhooks wondering just what is going to happen next. Unfinished business.

Pavlov's dogs

The behavioural psychology study of the Pavlovian Effect or Classical Conditioning, was conducted by Russian physiologist Ivan Pavlov.

His study at the time was in measuring the salivation rates of dogs produced in response to being fed. What he observed was that his dogs would begin to salivate whenever he entered the room, regardless of whether he had food or not.

off the mark .com   by Mark Parisi

BELL RINGS, I GET A TREAT... BELL RINGS, I GET A TREAT... IT WENT ON THAT WAY FOR DAYS. THEN, OUT OF THE BLUE ... BELL RINGS, I GET **NOTHING AT ALL!!** NADA! I MEAN, CAN YOU SERIOUSLY CALL MY ATTACK UNPROVOKED?

THE DARK TRUTH ABOUT PAVLOV'S DOG.

He recognised that it was an inherent behaviour for the dogs to salivate when presented with food; that it was not a learned behaviour but an instinct or natural response for a dog to experience increased salivation at the smell or sight of food, as salivation aids in digestion.

What he deduced from this observation was that the dogs had learned to associate his presence with food.

He further tested the theory by introducing another neutral stimulus, this time being a bell. He started by ringing a bell and measuring the amount of saliva produced by the dogs when they heard it – the results reflected no increased response from the dogs.

He then introduced ringing the bell each time he fed the dogs, after repeating this several times (ringing the bell and feeding the dogs), he then only rang the bell.

This time the results reflected increased salivation when the dogs heard a bell, because the dogs had learned to associate the sound of a bell with being fed.

How I tested Pavlov's theory

I first became aware of this psychological concept about 15 years ago when one of my professional peers Dinesh Prasad likened one of my daily jobs to the 'Pavlov's dog' experiment.

I still laugh quietly to myself when I recall the conversation, because the humour and context applied in his passing comment is still relevant and I still see it every day.

Early in my career being a young office administrator, one of the responsibilities that I had was at morning teatime, where it was my job to collect from a **locked** cupboard **one** packet of Family Assorted biscuits, for employees to enjoy with their morning tea or coffee.

Another one of my peers Marian likened the daily morning tea experience to a scene in the movie *Jurassic Park*, when the camera focused on a velociraptor dragging their nails across the stainless-steel benchtop in the kitchen where those terrified kids were hiding. Her hilarious visual prompt still sets a laugh trigger for me.

I laugh, because one 500 gram packet of Family Assorted biscuits contains approximately 50 biscuits. How this relates to Dinesh's association with 'Pavlov's dog's' was that at the time there were approximately 50 staff working for the company.

Easy math reflects that the allocation of one packet of biscuits equates to one biscuit per employee. But what happens when one employee partakes in more than one biscuit? What happens is that Pavlovian Conditioning becomes evident in the workplace.

I laugh out loud when I recall the rush of bodies that flooded the office kitchenette at 10.00 am, when they responded to the rustle I made whilst opening the packet of biscuits.

For the laugh and to test the theory, I would occasionally collect the packet of biscuits from the locked cupboard at 9.30 am and place them quietly on the bench. I would then return to the kitchenette at 10.00 am to see if anyone had opened the packet of biscuits.

Often, the packet of biscuits would be in the same condition I had placed it in – unopened and unviolated.

Occasionally, someone would place their own need for gratification (or hunger) above the needs of others and would open the packet of biscuits – probably figuring that the risk to themselves in opening the biscuits prior to the designated morning teatime was weighted against their own benefit and to that end justifiable.

What I observed was that if someone had the temerity to open the packet of biscuits before 10.00 am there were few, if any, biscuits left in the biscuit tray for consumption at the designated morning tea break.

From this I recognised, that regardless of whether I opened the packet of biscuits or not, regardless of the company established time of 10.00 am for a morning tea break, as soon as someone heard the rustle of a biscuit packet being opened, a migration of staff occurred within the office.

It is perhaps an overshare and an indication of my somewhat wicked sense of humour – but I still recall vividly, the howls of indignation resonating from the company kitchenette at 10.00 am, if all the biscuits were gone. *Rolling on the floor killing myself laughing right now…*

One thing I ascertained for sure, was that Pavlov's Theory appeared sound, because as the rustle of commercial food packaging resounded across the floor – a flood of engineering and drafting staff would respond to what they knew would lead to something that would somewhat satiate their appetite until lunchtime.

I don't want you to think that the company that I worked for was in any way stingy in the allocation of the morning titbit they provided to their employees, it's just that no one had given thought to providing more biscuits as the workforce grew.

Be assured and enjoy peaceful slumber in knowing that after my fun (and short) informal study of 'Pavlov's Theory' concluded, three packets of biscuits were provided to the workforce at morning tea time to accommodate the gluttons and the people who found themselves late to the feast because the location of their workstation in the office was farthest from the kitchenette.

RUGBY Quality Review in a nutshell

Using these two scientific studies of behaviour, **RUGBY Quality Review provides a visual cue that has been placed to stimulate a particular response** – *that being recognising that the task is not completed.*

By placing a red, green, blue or yellow tag you are promoting a continual review and improvement loop, which should capture change as it occurs in your business or upon review of your business process and procedures.

> *"RUGBY Quality Review provides a visual cue that has been placed to stimulate a particular response – that being recognising that the task is not completed."*
>
> **Katrina Wilson**

CHAPTER 23

Monumental ****-Ups

Contrary to the chapter heading, this chapter is not about mistakes. This chapter is about our human response to error and how we can easily overlook significant risk in our business because of our perception of how our business operates.

This share is a reluctant share because I have a huge affection for the person who identified this mistake as a 'monumental ****-up'. It's an important share however, because it was this experience that ultimately contributed to the cohesion of RUGBY Mindset and RUGBY Quality Review.

I'm not going to share too much information as to what the mistakes were either – because it's not my business. This is why this chapter is not about the mistake but rather the risk and response.

To protect the integrity of the person that I hold affection for – you need only know the following:

- The process failure became evident within the opening weeks of my employment.

- It was a hard failure and not a soft failure, because the mistake could not be reversed or moderated.

It was the night before Christmas eve that I (and my employer) became aware of the mistake. I spent a sleepless night because I could not identify how I had made the mistake. I spent a sleepless night because the mistake that had been made, transposed from a profit to a loss – and I felt sick about it.

I spent a sleepless night because I knew the next day I would be attending the office to be on the unpleasant side of the business equivalent to a smacked bottom. A mistake had occurred and I was responsible for it.

At this time, Christmas did not seem something much to celebrate – certainly my employer was hard hit and I could not see me finding my way onto his 'gift list'.

It was not until I was half an hour away from presenting myself to the office that I asked myself, "Am I solely responsible for the mistake or did I contribute towards the mistake?" Up until this point, until I asked myself this question, I was holding myself responsible for the mistake – without doubt, my employer was doing the same in thinking that the new girl had made a stupid mistake that had cost their business money.

Throughout the previous sleepless night and my time spent in transit to the office, I had been asking myself "What did I do wrong?" I did not ask myself "How did this happen?"

By asking myself "How did this happen?" I consciously repositioned myself from the position of being accountable and responsible for the error, to questioning how I had contributed to the mistake.

By asking this question, I was looking to identify the point of origin of where the failure occurred – not what I did wrong.

In doing so I transitioned from a 'victim mentality', where I expected to be reprimanded with responsibility placed firmly at my door, to a 'victor mentality', where I expected to be reprimanded with responsibility correctly identified and assigned against all doors. *I was presenting myself to my employer as part of the solution and not the problem.*

It was with significant relief that I realised that I had in fact not done anything wrong and that I was not solely responsible for the mistake – and I knew this, because I had followed the procedure the business had in place for the work to be delivered against.

Checks and balances were in place in this business, the correct process had been followed – and yet the mistake still occurred. This is why I verbally agreed wholeheartedly with my then employer, that this indeed was a monumental ****-up when he termed the phrase upon entering the office and eyeballing me.

What I realised half an hour away from the office, was that the mistake had occurred because the information that I had and was working from was incorrect. At some point, something had changed in the way the business was conducted as it grew and it had not been captured when the change occurred.

I also recognised belatedly that the most significant unrecognised contributing risk that any employer or business is exposed to had not been appropriately identified either by myself or my employer. What was the significant risk? That a new employee had entered an unfamiliar territory, that there was a new player on the field to do the work that someone else had done before.

A new employee who had no knowledge that the way the work had been completed previously had changed, therefore an employee who was not in a position to identify that their work was incorrect.

This is why employers hate losing competent employees – because the most significant risk and cost when an employee leaves, is lost through the knowledge and experience the employee has to how the business is conducted and it is for this very reason that RUGBY Quality Review will support your business.

The experience and information of a departing employee is rarely passed on, as the new employee is usually employed with little or no opportunity for handover – and is something that I recognised, addressed and put in place before I left this employer. *Throughout my employment, I nurtured a living document, which I called my succession plan.*

It was a living document, which captured every responsibility and deliverable I had in the role and all the critical information that I had captured as I did my job. I developed and put this in place to not only support my employer but to also support the next person who was going to be responsible for the job.

I identified this succession plan as a critical document for review and it was updated as something changed or as something new occurred and it was reviewed every month.

Where I gave some thought to the benefits of RUGBY Quality Review was in recognising that as soon as I was no longer employed in that company – the document had potential to never be reviewed again. It's probably now defunct.

It was with some relief that I identified where the point of failure occurred, not only to save my own business hide from a proverbial tanning, but because regrettable as the mistake was there were lessons learned and things that could be done to mitigate the same mistake from occurring again – albeit a hard lesson for my employer.

It was this experience that ultimately captured what a RUGBY Mindset has been developed to recognise, that every person involved in a business contributes to the ***success or failure*** of the business from the spectrum of either being accountable, responsible, contributing or informed.

One final question. How does one differentiate between a mistake and a monumental ****-up? What is the scale between the two? Whilst I was working in South Korea, I became acutely aware of the Deep Water Horizon incident in 2010 – because I was working as part of a team who were constructing a deep water semisubmersible drilling rig.

This human and environmental tragedy changed from something that I was peripherally aware of because of news reports, to something that I (and every person I was working with in South Korea) was very well informed about, because the Deepwater Horizon rig, like the projects we were working on – was designed, built and operated by humans – all of whom, at some point may have demonstrated some human agency which would have contributed towards the catastrophe.

This catastrophe killed 11 people, contributed to an environmental disaster and cost the owner billions of dollars, I'll leave you to draw your own conclusion of exactly where this event would sit on the scale between a mistake and a monumental ****-up.

> *"Monumental ****-ups are subjective because our context affects the experience."*
>
> **Katrina Wilson**

CHAPTER 24

Our Perception of Failure

Failures should never be about blame (although they almost always are); failures should always be about identifying the point of origin to eliminate the potential for the

same mistake being made in the future (although they almost never are).

As humans, we all make mistakes. Some of us make mistakes and learn from them and some of us continue to make the same mistakes. Songs have been written!

This chapter has been written with thought to the people out there in the world who think that not only do they **not** make mistakes, but also it is their right – perhaps with some twisted logic towards creating a superior race – to browbeat the poor unfortunate that actually has to work with them.

For all people who believe in a business utopia where mistakes do not exist, I have five words. Stop! Please… *I beg you*. Not only are you aspiring to something that has never existed, but through your words and negative attention, you are:

- Actively contributing towards a toxic and therefore unhealthy milieu.

- Isolating a human's natural response to reflect and learn from a mistake, self-regulate and take responsibility.

- Restricting potential to recognise and respond appropriately to the mistake; to ensure that the mistake doesn't occur again.

- Halting any opportunity a person may take to innovate, learn or develop in the workplace, which could turn to profit for a business.

- Effectively demonstrating the physical equivalent of removing your steel-capped boot, high heel or loafer, taking it in hand and then smacking someone around the head with it – which is something that would never be tolerated in a healthy environment. Not only is it reprehensible, it serves no purpose – so why do it?

For all the people who want to work towards establishing a business utopia, where mistakes are recognised and responded to comprehensively, I would suggest that you use your admirable powers of observation – your ability to look for and find fault – for good.

If you look to find fault, you will find it. Arson investigators look to find evidence of arson, not evidence of a fire. Fire investigators look to find evidence to identify the source of a fire. Forensic crash units look to find the contributing factors of motor vehicle accidents. In the most part, people look to find fault **because something bad happened and they want someone to blame**.

RUGBY Quality Review promotes the opportunity to look to find fault and positively respond to it.

Positively netted, mistakes present an opportunity for a business to gain a competitive edge and opportunity to benefit and profit, if their employees are confidently supported to look to find fault; *and not use it to place blame or assign it against another's character.*

Looking to find fault can be a profitable exercise if you use the information or the potential failure that you have found for good, as it may:

- Bring focus to address a wider issue that has until this time been hidden, unidentified or unrecognised in your business.

- Identify the potential a person or a business may be exposed to unnecessary risk.

- Improve, innovate or eliminate a business practice that no longer suits a business's model.

- Provide opportunity to break down the silos that exist in business by sharing information and opportunities.

- Develop and expand on a person's skill base and knowledge.

> *"Positively netted, mistakes present an opportunity for a business to gain a competitive edge and opportunity to benefit and profit, if their employees are confidently supported to look to find fault; **and not use it to place blame or assign it against another's character.**"*
>
> **Katrina Wilson**

SECTION 4

Norming

CHAPTER 25

Capturing and Assigning Value to Your Time

You may recall I mentioned that for the early half of 2015 I found myself with a little time on my hands? It was during this time, that I gave a thought to developing RUGBY Quality Review and it was also the time that I spent in trying to identify what my personal point of difference could be. The things that would make me stand out from the other candidates that I was competing against as I was trying to find paid employment.

The first thing that I noted, was that my own skillset was probably in line with the skillset of others – so there was nothing unique about that to contribute into the workplace. *A person's skillset is what they are employed to use to support a business.*

My point of difference was identified through reflection. It was in looking back upon my scattered and global employment history, where I spent some time invested in fondly recalling the amazing major project exposure and some of the exceptional people that I had worked with.

I was provided the opportunity to not only be a little grateful for the challenges I had experienced, but to identify how I now shape as a professional because I realised that I had not just been employed for my skillset. My skillset was no more impressive than another's was – anyone could do the job I did on these projects.

I was employed, because the person who employed me recognised that I had a resilient character and the discipline to mindfully choose my response — *this is what makes me unique in business.*

I am employed not because my curriculum vitae reflects working on major, billion dollar projects both in Australia and in South Korea. I am employed, because working on these projects, with the project workload and the stress associated to it, necessitated that I get efficient, productive and exceptional with my focus and skillset and as a result has enhanced my ability to deliver on any job that I am employed to deliver.

I have enhanced my skillset because I take the time to recognise the two things that consume the most of my time, and it is probably the two things that consume most of your time in the workplace. They are:

- Our human decision to work on the things that we like to work on first, leaving the less desirable deliverables to work on last or *never*.

- Managing our inbox. Navigating through the quagmire of our inbox and balancing our to-do list.

To manage these two things I have developed two skills. The first being 'baton touch' and the second being making my inbox something that works **for me**.

Baton touch

To improve *my* efficiency, and to limit my propensity to work on the fun stuff first, I disciplined myself to develop the habit to *only touch something once*. If I had something that I needed to work on – I focused on that one task and completed everything that needed to be completed on it – before I either closed it out or forwarded it on to someone else for further action. A baton touch.

This sweet little turn of phrase I picked up while working in South Korea, one night whilst watching free-to-air television no less. I watched free-to-air television so I could pick up the Korean language and get a little familiar with its culture. It's amazing what you can pick up in watching a serial on television, even though you don't understand a lick of the language – because, you respond to what you are viewing and you respond to the music that is being played.

On this Korean serial, baton touch was referred to promote shift work, the seamless pass from one shift to another – and it got me curious, not only because of the time I spent in trying to translate and understand what I had just viewed, it got me curious because it so beautifully captures what every business looks to achieve, an ability to seamlessly deliver.

Emails

*One of the most important things to remember about your inbox is that it is a business tool – that requires a little human agency to really get it working **for** you.*

Most of our work deliverables, instructions and communications are received nowadays by electronic mail – and I applied the discipline of baton touch to manage my inbox as well.

This meant that I disciplined myself to form the habit to not pick and choose what I was going to work on from the emails in my inbox – I do not give myself the luxury of not working on something because it was not something that I enjoyed doing.

Using a baton touch, I touch an email once, I work on the deliverables and once complete *I **immediately** move the email **out** of my inbox* into a folder which I title 'actioned items'.

This discipline is my key to managing my inbox, because the only thing I want in my inbox are the emails that I have something to deliver on.

Once you no longer have something to contribute, *you move* that email out of your inbox – thereby harnessing the great strength found in the Zeigarnik effect. You move on to what your required focus **is** and move away from the information or tasks that no longer require your attention.

Identifying the value of your time

"Can't you see I'm busy?"

This brief sub-chapter, captures what I alluded to in the opening chapters of this book where I identified the second gold nugget that fell out of my authorship experience, whilst I was interrogating how the disciplines of RUGBY Quality Review could support a business and its quality focus.

It actually started as a little bit of fun, where I sought to place my own measure and value of my time spent in the workplace, against the deliverables I was accountable and paid to deliver on, for both my employer and myself.

For fun, I sought to identify a quantifiable value on the investment made by my employer against my presence as an employee or contractor and how I delivered on my work as an evaluator.

You can see in the following graph:

- If one person was paid a day rate of $300 and completed their work in eight hours, their hourly rate of pay reflects as $38 per hour.

- You can also see that if one person (an evaluator) was paid a day rate of $300 and completed their work in one hour, their hourly rate of pay reflects as $300 per hour.

- Regardless of whether you work eight hours or one hour per day – the amount of money taken home is the same, $300 per day.

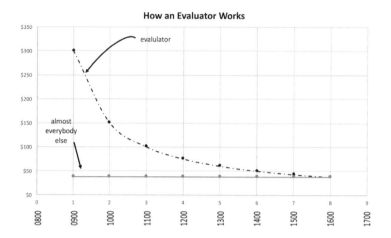

The graph below captures what my colleague and friend Donna and I both know – if we can capture time in our day to profit, we can assist others if they need a helping hand or we can develop our skillset, attend training or conduct research that will support us in our roles.

Everyone has the potential to work within this focus and framework because people get very good at things with a little bit of focus and practice.

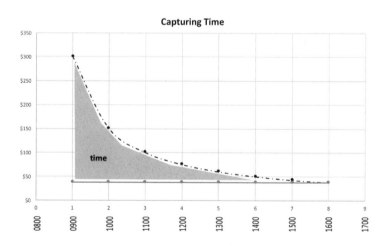

How does an evaluator's approach capture as a profit for our employers? Our employers have access to a resource or employee who has the discipline, potential and capacity to work with the efficiency of two or three employees.

> *"People get very good at things with a little bit of focus and practice."*
>
> **Katrina Wilson**

SECTION 5

Performing

CHAPTER 26

The Inverse Lottery

The author is grateful to Delena Brophy Farmer and Paul Blackburn for contributing towards this, probably the most important chapter.

Everyone knows what a lottery is. It's a situation whose success or outcome is determined by chance and it is also a legalised form of gambling – a drawing of lots if you will, in which prizes are distributed to the winners among persons **buying a chance**.

The wonderful thing about a lottery is that you can opt in to being a potential winner or victor – simply by purchasing a ticket. You are in it – so there is potential that you can win it.

Conversely you can opt out of participating – simply by not purchasing a ticket. In doing so you have removed the potential to neither win something nor lose something. Your position remains neutral – unless you consider an opportunity cost. But that's a whole other chapter!

I started to think of safety and quality and the symbiotic relationships between the two because RUGBY Quality Review has been developed and massaged from a successful site safety practice. There are many similarities between both safety and quality with the common and most obvious contributor being, **risk**. How we recognise and respond to a business or a person's potential to be exposed to risk and all her casualties.

I started to draw parallels from a lottery focus because it is how we humans respond to safety and quality. *We play the odds.* We play the odds of something changing or not changing and we weight those odds pretty heavily towards 'one in a million'.

With safety and safety management practices, we mortals calculate quickly, and without conscious thought, what we consider to be the potential for an unsafe work practice, act or behaviour, to result in lost time, injury or death. What we then do is consider the potential of being on the receiving end of the business equivalent of a slap across the face or being identified as an agitator, if we do get involved.

We consider all of these things and then we apply some personal logic and odds to weight our response which is usually something along the lines of '*the likelihood of something bad happening is less likely to occur than the negative attention I will receive by doing something*'.

With quality and quality management practices, we don't calculate at all. We continue to use the same practices and perhaps tired formula, which we have associated to success (and not failure) since time immemorial, simply because it's the way we've always worked. We don't challenge the status quo because the status quo is most comfortable without challenge.

The thought of an Inverse Lottery to capture the parallels between safety and quality, came about because I made the observation that in *both* safety and quality any one person, any one business *does not* have the luxury of choice in either opting in to a lottery, *by purchasing a ticket*, or opting out of a lottery, *by **not** purchasing a ticket*.

With an Inverse Lottery, a person or business does not get to choose if they are involved on not involved in a quality or safety issue, because even if they think they have opted out simply by not opting in – ***someone else has already bought them a ticket in the Inverse Lottery*** – because they too think they have opted out simply by not opting in.

As an example from a safety perspective, if someone walks past an unsafe work practice or hazard without stopping the work or isolating the hazard – they are buying not only their own ticket in the Inverse Lottery – they are buying *more than one other person*, a ticket in the Inverse Lottery. It's the same with quality.

The more tickets you either buy yourself, or someone else buys for you in an Inverse Lottery, the better the chances that one day your numbers are going to come up, *in a lottery that you never want to win*.

Why should we focus on safety?

Paul Blackburn

When Katrina first approached me to contribute in this book, I was intrigued. After all, everybody knows that safety and quality are two sides of the one coin in business and a constant challenge for any business owner or safety and quality professional.

I was curious to see how she would match and marry the two disciplines, safety and quality, and I've not been disappointed because she shared in our conversations an interesting concept, one that looked towards identifying and addressing the behaviours and considerations that challenge our success in embracing mindful and safe work practices, and mindful quality work practices in the workplace.

Her concept is one of 'Inverse Lottery', the lottery that **no one wants to win**.

Why should we focus on safety? The most obvious answer to this is to ensure that we return home from our job, to our loved ones and friends, in sound health at the end of every day or shift.

Safety is a word that conjures up a myriad of responses from people for an infinite number of reasons. The description of safety, mindful safe work practices and the evidence based safety management systems as a lottery, with particular focus towards an *Inverse Lottery*, is classically captured because it recognises at the basic root or primary level, how humans respond to safety and quality. *We play the odds.* We calculate quickly what we consider to be the potential for an unsafe work practice, act or behaviour to have a negative effect.

The idea of safety as an Inverse Lottery presents a situation in which we are placing our personal health and wellbeing in the hands of others *and* change, and sincerely hoping that when that Inverse Lottery is figuratively drawn, that *our number is not drawn out.*

A Safety Management System (SMS) is a common method used by a business or organisation to capture the manner, process and systems to support the fundamental concept of safety.

If an organisation has nil, little or limited safety management systems in place, it could indeed represent a lottery for employees, who are staying safe through luck rather than good management.

Of course, employees expect more protection from harm whilst undertaking employment, and this is mandated through various pieces of legislation. *What may surprise many organisations and employers is the actual effectiveness of their respective safety management systems.*

Let's start by asking "how do we describe or define safety?" Anywhere from paperwork or red tape – something that is considered an obstruction or interference with a person's ability to do their job, all the way across the spectrum to being embraced as a passionate rhetoric which borders on manic obsession. The balance and the success of safe work attitudes and practices sits somewhere close to the middle.

The requirement of an employee to be provided with a safe place of work is enshrined in Australian Law and captured in its Acts and Regulations. The focus and deliberate attention paid to work safety related aspects has increased exponentially since its inception in the early 1800s.

There is a fundamental agreement in business that with the concept of safety – in that people should not expect to be injured or suffer illness through the course of their employment.

There *isn't* a fundamental agreement in relation to the manner, process and systems that can, could, should or may possibly be implemented to achieve this concept of safety. This is something that is tailored to uniquely capture and manage all potential risk that a business or organisation and its employees or contracting parties may be exposed to and it reflects as a safety management system.

A safety management system can be found in many forms, with various names and providing differing levels of success.

The common denominator across these safety management systems is, or should be, *the focus on the risk reduction and management in relation to human beings*. There are most certainly environmental, business continuity and reputational elements to many of these systems – but it's called a Safety Management System for a reason – it's a primary tool for a business or organisation to reduce risk to employees.

Where safety's behaviour and message gets blurry is when a safety management system is considered and structured as a high level, strategic and corporate (read: head office) document and not for the intent and purpose it was developed to support – *the people who are specifically undertaking the actual tasks which may have risk associated with them.*

In order to be successful in the core function of reducing risk to employees, a safety management system must have the ability to engage those employees. If the tone, language, structure or expectations of a document are beyond the target audience, then the success of the safety management system will likely falter or fail.

Being user-friendly and consistent with industry best practice and actual organisational expectations is crucial to a safety management system being taken up and used as intended. With regrettable regularity, I note that safety management systems are too often written towards corporate and audit audiences and as such are not transparently and comprehensively understood by the work crews who are required to comply with them and leads to a safety management system not being used for its original actual intended purpose.

When a safety management system is not used for its intended purpose, someone has just purchased a ticket in the Inverse Lottery.

When a safety management system is not followed, employees are not being protected by the systems, processes and practices that have been put in place by their respective employer, thereby leaving themselves exposed to the world of luck, chance and the Inverse Lottery. In the world of luck, chance and the Inverse Lottery, employees are making decisions for themselves, without clear expectations, unsupported by risk management processes and in many cases far from any element of best practice.

This Inverse Lottery world may also exist within organisations that have a safety management system which is not utilised by employees for varying reasons, such as condoned practices, lack of engagement or knowledge. It's left on a shelf somewhere and rarely dusted off.

This is where I think Kat's idea of RUGBY Mindset and Quality Review will reinvigorate how we focus our attention and support our people in safety. In setting a review cadence that suits the individual needs of each business and providing visual cues that require attention and response. In using RUGBY, it would be quite possible and a surprisingly simple process for a business or organisation to move from a world of an Inverse Lottery to one of engaged compliance.

Why should we focus on quality?

Delena Brophy Farmer

What are the odds of that happening?

That'll never happen to me!

We'll cross that bridge when we come to it.

These are all common phrases we use every day. Seemingly innocent in their meaning but serious consequences often result from an event that could have been prevented. Sometimes the outcome is small, sometimes the outcome is catastrophic.

In all cases, there are things that could have been done to mitigate the risk of loss. This is also known as taking a ticket in the Inverse Lottery.

We unwittingly buy tickets to the Inverse Lottery each and every day. If you were to sit down at the beginning of each day and do a risk assessment about the forthcoming day, you would be shocked at what you find. Potentially you would not leave the house!

Just as in day to day life, we make decisions based on the information we have or think we have. When running a business there are many factors that come into play. Other people making decisions that may or may not be in line with the focus of the business. Information that is not known at the specific time. Or something as simple as someone didn't care enough to pay attention to what could happen. They've just bought a ticket to the Inverse Lottery.

Most people dream of the day they win the lottery – what I could do with that money, how that money could provide my family and friends with a better life and I could set myself up for the rest of my life. If you really analyse the odds, you probably wouldn't bother to buy a ticket but millions of dollars are spent on 'the dream' that is the lottery.

Running a business, any sort of business, any size of business, is dependent upon the people who are contributing to it. Unlike the lottery where people buy a chance to win the prize, employees who are contributing to a business are not just buying a ticket. They have been chosen for the role because they meet a certain criteria and they are expected to meet their deliverables.

This applies to all aspects of running a business, but none more crucial then when it comes to safety and quality management. Safety is about the human risk and quality is about financial risk. Both can be viewed as inverse lotteries.

So, something slips in quality, what is the worst that can happen? A financial loss may occur or a contractual obligation may not be fulfilled. When something slips in safety then the worst thing could be that someone may not make it home to their family.

The size of the business should not dictate the level of safety or quality management that should be in place. A small business may become a big business in a very short time and the need for systems and processes, if in place from the beginning, will support the growth as it occurs. Most businesses experience organic growth and the business owner is always looking for a way to land that big contract or become a part of a larger supply chain to its sector. More tickets to the Inverse Lottery.

Take the manufacturing sector. They produce a product to meet the client's needs but it also must meet certain Standards. Standards that have been written to protect something or someone. A great example of this is ISO Standards. Globally recognised minimum standards that businesses adopt to ensure that they are meeting an expectation and ultimately delivering the same outcome each and every time.

Safety and Quality Management Systems exist because somewhere in the past, there have been many instances where there was a lack of minimum standards and a loss occurred. Many times, this was in the form of human life.

Industries that are identified as high risk have the added challenge that is legislation. Regulators, rightly or wrongly, legislate to protect those who can't always protect themselves. This in turn often creates additional burden on business that is seen to be unnecessary and expensive. Failure to meet this is more tickets in the Inverse Lottery.

Until their number comes up. That day when there is an accident on site or a product is manufactured and sold to the public and because it didn't meet the Standard, it has injured or killed the end user. That's an Inverse Lottery win that no one wants.

Remember, that statement, "That'll never happen to us!"

There are thousands of pages of court documents that tell a different story. Spend an afternoon looking through case law relating to workplace deaths and you suddenly see, that, had systems and process been in place, followed, reviewed and updated, that many of these tragedies may have been prevented. Some are just simply tragedies that too many variables meant that it would have been hard to prevent.

Businesses look to mitigate potential losses in various ways. Insurance, marketing, sales and manufacturing a product are all ways business mitigate or control risk.

Some may feel that sales and marketing is not as important as the product that they manufacture, but in reality, if sales and marketing are not maintaining their focus and following their plan, then there may not be sales of the product that the manufacturing arm is producing, the age old philosophy of supply and demand.

Many feel comfort that comes with having an insurance policy in place that will protect them should something go wrong. It's a paradox, no one wants to pay for it, but they are pleased they have it when they need it.

Well-designed systems can be viewed in the same light as having an insurance policy. Periodically – normally once a year – you review your insurance cover to see whether or not it will meet your needs for the coming year. You take into account any claims you may have had and any new items that may need to be covered by the policy.

Management systems are the same. Periodically, key parts need to be reviewed to ensure that they are meeting the objectives of the business at that time. By not having a management system in place, then you are relying on the chance that your numbers won't come up or if they do, that's when you will conduct a review.

Sometimes, risks can remain hidden and unchecked without ever revealing themselves. Out of sight out of mind. Sometimes, however, a known risk may be overlooked as the potential loss may be seen by someone as a small casualty.

This often comes down to the decision of one individual. If that individual is the owner of the business, then that may be acceptable, but when that individual is a paid employee, then the fallout of their actions may have a ripple effect.

The importance of having a system in place is that it doesn't matter who is performing what tasks, the same standard will be delivered no matter what.

This is all well and good, but if you don't have a robust system in place then this is something that simply can't happen.

What does a robust system look like? Where do I get a system like that? Can I buy one off the shelf? What if I can't afford to pay for a system?

Introducing a management system into your business is like buying that winning lottery ticket. No one wants to buy an Inverse Lottery ticket with the 'win' reflecting a massive loss – financial loss or loss of life.

Management systems need to be fit for purpose, just like any other equipment used in your business. They must reflect the needs of your business and not be taken from someone else's business that isn't fit for purpose.

If you try to adopt someone else's system or documentation in your own business and it doesn't fit, then you are at risk of compounding the problem. The problem is often compounded because everyone thinks that the system is covering them, when it's actually failing them more than not having a system at all.

Implementing a system that is simple in its structure but complex in its deliverables is important. If something is too difficult, then it's often left until it becomes a critical issue.

Don't set out to be the winner of the Inverse Lottery because you don't know what you're doing or where to start. Small business should adopt big business thinking and start developing a robust system to protect the livelihood and success for all stakeholders.

Early adopters will often reap the rewards because they saw the potential before anyone else. A competitive edge becomes a streamlined business unit or simply that it makes good business sense to have a system so you can reproduce the same product or service day in day out and capitalise on the savings this brings.

The RUGBY Quality Review is the perfect starting point to allow you to understand the needs of your business before embarking on trying to implement a management system that may not support the structure and objectives of your business.

RUGBY Quality Review is a proven and robust system as it has already been demonstrated by how successfully it has been used on site not only to identify risk but for people to respond to the visual cues that contribute towards a safe and healthy workplace.

RUGBY's Mindset and unique use of technology will not only reduce the gap between acceptable and unacceptable risk in your business, it will also increase the potential for a business to tap into new opportunities all the while using your existing collateral and stakeholders.

CHAPTER 27

Your Superior Playbook

There are many contributing factors to how I thought of and then developed RUGBY Quality Review – taken from my own observations and experiences in the workplace.

RUGBY Quality Review started because I recognised why quality review and practices are so essential in business and identified the cost to business when quality and the opportunity to review are overlooked.

Quality is important because many businesses work towards capturing the recognition of certifying their quality practices with external bodies and to internationally recognised standards. Standards, which have been developed, because there was a need to define and provide an internationally recognised consistent baseline to be certified against.

But I also realised, that whilst quality and review is important to business its importance is not recognised as strongly by the people employed within a business. Unless your role title reflects: Director Quality or Quality Manager.

When an employee doesn't recognise or place the same value against quality review and continual improvement that a business requires for compliance and sustainability, a business has workplace conflict and exposure to financial loss and business risk.

Quality is an ugly baby. The point I am trying to make is not that a baby IS ugly – but that other people have their own perception of what ugly is.

In the true sense of the statement, if someone walked up to a mother or father and stated that their baby was ugly – they would not only think that the person was rude for having said that in the first place, they would be hurt and would defend, not only their baby but themselves, because they believe the statement to be *intrusive and false.*

No one wants to receive the unsolicited observation that their baby is ugly – and in a parent's eyes, a baby is only ever beautiful.

Why quality is an ugly baby is for the same reason. Someone in the workplace has identified potential for the work or contribution of another as 'ugly'. People don't want to hear that a business form, process or alignment no longer fits with the way the business is conducted. *They will defend their baby and they will defend themselves.*

They don't want to hear that with a little time and nurturing, a quality review conducted with integrity, could bring about improvements, profit, potential to reassess business risk and positive change – because they are comfortable in their work, in the way that they work – they don't think their work needs attention, and they will defend themselves and their work because they believe the statement of be intrusive and false.

The whole purpose of quality review and quality practices is to identify if the current process and practice of your business is best practice and compliant to the way you have identified that your business is conducted. The benefit of effective quality review and quality practices is that you have the potential to not only improve, you have the potential to exceed and position yourself and your business with a competitive edge.

This is what quality auditors do, when they come into your business to conduct an audit. They look to find that you, your employees and your business:

- Are conducting your business in the way that you have identified and received your ISO accreditation against.

- Have periodically reviewed your business process and procedure to not only ensure that you are compliantly delivering against your ISO accreditation but also capturing change and making improvements.

So why is quality review and its purpose so hard to harness and address, if quality review is such an important part of business to:

- Capture change and make improvements?

- Mitigate exposure to risk and financial loss?

- Evidence to support accreditation against international standards *the minimum standard that is required to be achieved*?

- Identify potential and a competitive edge for efficiencies to occur and other areas of a business to profit?

I think I have an answer and solution. We struggle to properly embrace quality and quality review practices, because we don't have a superior playbook.

Before I embarked on my major projects experiences, I worked for a short time with a legal firm in Brisbane – which was an interesting segue from where I had come from working in consulting design engineering and the legal exposure I had whilst working for them.

Working with a law firm, allowed me to recognise that the strategies that legal specialists use as they work to build their case for their clients were not that far removed from the strategies, checks and balances that successful businesses consider and deploy, because the legal fraternity have milestone dates and evidences that must be produced within that frame, for a legal case to *proceed*.

It was in the first week of working with this firm, that I was handed a book to read. I remember thinking at the time, "I don't want to read a book." I didn't want to read a book because I was fired up and keen, as all new employees are fired up and keen, to effect some change, which sounds like a positive, but if you look at it from the perspective of others, being fired up and keen could be interpreted as just another new person in the company looking to imprint their will on another.

The book I was handed to read was a gift similar in its giving, to the gift I had received from Bill and Alison with *The Art of War for Women*. Someone was gifting to me something that they considered would be a valuable contribution to my success.

This book, *Mastering the Rockefeller Habits* by Verne Harnish, was a book that every single employee of that firm had access to. It was a gift, because what I was being handed that day, was a pause in my own ambitions and an introduction to the vernacular of that firm.

Contained within those pages were the primary position and mindset from which the firm, and everyone employed within it, conducted it-or-themselves, and as such, it was the way the owners of that firm recognised the success and professional conduct of its employees, the behaviours that would attribute to the firms success for their clients (which was their primary focus) and its growth.

Unknown to myself at the time, the material promoted within this business 'playbook' assisted me in my transition to working FIFO because many of the business disciplines and rigours this book promoted are similar to those used on major construction projects.

I strongly encourage you to spend some time in developing your business's superior playbook.

If this book is not an example of how your business can re-pioneer its quality focus, its corporate behaviours and the behaviours of your employees, required to support your vision and success, *then please make the effort to develop your own competitive edge* by pulling together a superior playbook that will support you, your business and your employees.

Author's Final Word

I hope that you find the concept of RUGBY Mindset as a unique and appealing practical solution towards reinvigorating a quality focus, continual improvement loop and a competitive edge, either in your business or as you develop yourself personally. I hope that it introduces a new vernacular from which you can start enjoying conversations within your workplaces that everyone will benefit from.

Take a moment to recognise that, like me, you might only be as smart as the person you sit beside, become situationally aware to your immediate environment and start reaping the benefits of a new growth mindset.

Challenge yourself personally to see opportunity where others see adversity and challenge yourself towards levelling that business playing field by contributing towards a workplace where failure is recognised and responded to responsibly and positively.

Remember that the business that makes the fewest mistakes is the one that gains the competitive edge – and a happier, healthier workplace.

Understand that the practical application of visual cues in quality using the RUGBY Quality Review process is only the first step towards strategic change.

RUGBY Quality Review is called RUGBY because the colours Red, Green, Blue and Yellow ('RGBY') are used as visual cues to provoke a response in your business; but more importantly, if requires ('U') contributing from somewhere in the middle of it for it to work properly.

You contributing from the middle of something are the solution to the challenges you face yourself personally and in your business – you just need to take that first confident step.

What's next for RUGBY? What we do next is a direct result of applying the one and only 'golden' foundation principle that RUGBY Mindset and Quality Review baselines from, which is '*a principle does not exist without a variable*'. Only one thing needs to change for everything to change.

It was in asking myself 'what is the one thing that could change RUGBY Quality Review from being an easily adopted and successful business practice to just another attempt to make quality a little sexier?'

You have probably already identified the potential point of failure if you have read a hard copy of this book. You can't respond appropriately to the visual cue of a red, green, blue or yellow tag identifier of RUGBY Quality Review – if you print a document in black and white, or if someone is colour-blind.

So RUGBY's next challenge was identified through the solution we found to address the one thing that could change everything. We are using marketing and technology to provide some next level thinking in the quality game – and it will be as easy as scanning the QR Code on the cover page of this book from your mobile phone.

One final rugby analogy. **The players move, not the spectators.**

Katrina

About the Author

Katrina Wilson is an international author, business and process administration specialist who demonstrates a keen focus towards evaluation in both her personal life and business. Which is what makes her contribution in business sometimes challenging and always unique.

A firm believer in displaying grace under pressure, at a young age she struck out on her own to travel and work in the United Kingdom. Not surprisingly, it was this experience that started to shape the adult and professional she is today. Not surprisingly, she found success. It was this experience that prepared her for her challenging and rewarding life.

She also believes that the best interest of an employee is served in having a mindset to protect, promote and preserve the best interest of their employer; because this attitude and behaviour will lead to developing an employee that every employer wants.

Katrina has received prestigious acknowledgments of her talents in the workplace. Whilst working in the United Kingdom she was the Midlands nominee for the national 'Temp of the Year' award with the recruitment company she was working through. Upon her return to Australia she was the recipient of the Office Professional of the Year award for the Darling Downs region of the Australian Institute of Office Professionals and a finalist in the Queensland state award the following year. And she was recipient of an AECOM Queensland 'Tunie' award attributed to demonstrated agility in the workplace.

Contributing to her many talents and skill base, she has worked with businesses and organisations that include AECOM, Shine Lawyers, Jacobs, MMG Limited, Horizon Resources International, Diamond Offshore Drilling, Thyssen Krupp and the University of Southern Queensland.

Katrina's professional affiliations include the USQ Women's Network at the University of Southern Queensland and her support of the 'Heart of Australia' health program which currently delivers essential health services to remote areas across South-East Queensland.

Through her authorship, it is Katrina's ambition to support and promote the 'Heart of Australia' specialist program in its vision to deliver revolutionary medical services across Australia.

She has worked across Australia, the United Kingdom and South Korea and has travelled throughout the United Kingdom, Ireland, Singapore, Malaysia, Indonesia, Thailand, New Zealand, South Korea and Japan.

Katrina Wilson is founder, creator and author of the RUGBY Mindset and Quality Review and lives in Queensland, Australia.

Recommended

Resources

Recommended Resources

Any talent with a defence background

By the time you get to this chapter of the book, you will likely have calculated that I have enjoyed the challenges and professional exposure of working with nine employers in 20 years. Some could say more jobs than hot dinners!

With these employers, through my roles and experiences, I have had the privilege of working with women and men who have inspired me and helped me to successfully deliver on the responsibilities I was employed to deliver on and achieve my own personal goals, through my own observations of their expertise and specialist capabilities and practical application of their shared experiences, training, discipline and education.

But I want to place particular focus to the lads and ladies who have been trained, educated, employed and deployed for both the Australian Defence Forces and the Australian Police Force.

It is the experiences and perspective that these people have shared with me, which has resulted in my radar pinging within a workplace, if I find out that someone with a defence or community liaison background is working in close proximity to my good self. Why? Because I want in! No way, this side of hell freezing over, am I going to leave the opportunity of an experience or a resource which I place value on to pass me by!

My radar pings because I **know** that these people have been educated by the best of the best, and are trained and disciplined to conceive, plan, execute and deliver.

Also, and I feel that this statement could feel a little bereft and left hanging following the previous sentence, also: it is my experience that the talent from the defence and community liaison contingent, care about the job that they do – which can often be overlooked or demoralised in business.

In short, these professionals know how to do their job and how to get the best result of what they are working on – all the while instilling confidence and focus for the people they are working with as they calmly deliver.

Of my professional peers, listed in the order of when I worked with them, who have experience with the Australian Defence Force I recommend, Mark Fairweather, Bill Thomson, Clint Verhagen, Justin Nally, Ryan Nally, Robbie Kirk, Neville Donohue, Belinda Reimers and Janine St Clair.

My only professional peer with experience working for an Australian Police Force and now applying his experience, passion and discipline as a safety specialist, Paul Blackburn.

Each and every one of the people I have identified above, has left an indelible mark on how I deliver on the work I am responsible for and approach business conversations, as well as shaping how I conduct myself both personally and in business.

I strongly recommend, that if you *ever* have the opportunity to enjoy working with, or just enjoy a conversation with, any of these amazing people – embrace it. You will challenge yourself to recalibrate your own personal and business compass and as an outcome be successful in what you focus on.

I extrapolate further in saying that my small defence and community liaison peerage, the people I have been privileged to work with and have been introduced to, represents a significant minority of the untapped talent that exists out there for businesses to profit from.

Do yourself and your business a favour by tapping into these resources.

Contributors

Dr John Knapton

John Knapton was Professor of Structural Engineering at University of Newcastle from 1991 to 2001, and has written a number of textbooks on the subject of concrete construction.

He has also worked as a consultant and expert witness in matters relating to concrete. These include a report for Lloyds' insurers on whether the design of the World Trade Center towers had contributed to their collapse on 9/11.

John is a highly esteemed international expert witness who specialises in concrete and asphalt pavements; structural engineering; aircraft, port and highway pavements; port, highway and aerodrome civil engineering structures; industrial floors, historic bridges; reinforced concrete; durability of concrete; concrete and brick pavers; permeable paving and sustainable drainage; slop stability and site investigations.

Dr Rolf Gomes

Heart of Australia is the brainchild of Brisbane cardiologist Dr Rolf Gomes, a father of three and the principal of Medihearts – his established private cardiology practice in Brisbane.

Rolf has committed his Medihearts practice to support the realisation of his vision for Heart of Australia – to revolutionise the delivery of first-class specialty services to rural and remote communities.

Mr Paul Blackburn

Paul Blackburn is a rescue, security and training specialist with a passion for contract management, industrial safety, emergency response and rescue, disaster management and security.

His operational experience captures across the Australian military and police force services as well as a fire fighter and mine site emergency response.

Paul's passions support his ability to provide practical and efficient training solutions for his clients to ensure that everyone is better positioned to return home safely at the end of a work day or shift.

Ms Delena Brophy Farmer

Delena Brophy Farmer is a seasoned professional in property, franchising, retail, manufacturing, management systems and standards.

Having worked for BSI Group (British Standards Institution), Delena is passionate about quality management and its importance for delivering sustainable and robust products, services and business longevity. She is extremely passionate about ISO Standards and their implementation into businesses, both large and small, where it is seen as a burden rather than an integral business function.

Delena also has over 20 years in the franchise sector working with both franchisors and franchisees in areas such as business development, recruitment, franchise resales, franchise renewals and business improvement. Delena assists small businesses in the development of targeted strategies to help them identify current and future opportunities using a variety of assessment and marketing streams.

Her experience brings together tools such as process improvement, territory mapping, demographic studies, franchise recruitment selection tools, standards writing and benchmarking to provide insight into planning and implementation of future potential growth strategies with science and data rather than gut feel.

Developing tools, processes and strategies to ensure that small businesses, franchisors and franchisees financial pathway is robust and will deliver measured outcomes consistently. With realistic tools and her clear communication style Delena ensure that all stakeholders understand the opportunities that exist for them.